Small Wonder

Small Wonder

A History of Small Point, Maine

TOM HINKLE

AMERICA THROUGH TIME®
ADDING COLOR TO AMERICAN HISTORY

America Through Time is an imprint of Fonthill Media LLC
www.through-time.com
office@through-time.com

Published by Arcadia Publishing by arrangement with Fonthill Media LLC
For all general information, please contact Arcadia Publishing:
Telephone: 843-853-2070
Fax: 843-853-0044
E-mail: sales@arcadiapublishing.com
For customer service and orders:
Toll-Free 1-888-313-2665

www.arcadiapublishing.com

First published 2020

ISBN 978-1-63499-257-2

Typeset in 10pt on 13pt Sabon
Printed and bound in England

Acknowledgments

I greatly appreciate the timing of this book—at the 200th anniversary of the state of Maine. Of course, the province of Maine was a thriving place for at least 200 years prior to its separation from the Massachusetts Bay Colony, and a considerable number of its citizens were opposed to the parting.

My history is not of the state but only of one small village—part of the coastal peninsula called Phippsburg. I was born in May, and in August, my parents transported me to their camp at Small Point, so I was not born in Maine. My history is partly a conventional one, partly my own. I knew many of the cast of characters.

I have not attempted to record the lives of all of Small Point's families; for a masterful genealogy, see Gloria Gray's two-volume *Small Point*. Gloria has published several large volumes of Phippsburg history and genealogy (she devotes eighty pages to Small Point's Wallace families); there is no competition as our histories go nicely together.

In addition to Gloria Gray, I have been greatly assisted by Carol Wyman Doughty, a direct descendant of Isaiah Wyman, an original settler, and a knowledgeable keeper of history; Gerald Wyman (who grew up in the Blaisdell Farmhouse); Sydney McDowell; Richard Lee; and State Historian Earle Shettleworth. Jack Ijams provided photographs of the Manley family that were taken by Sydney Manley. Abbie Sewall allowed me to use photographs by her great-grandmother, Emma Sewall. Elena Vandervoort helped with research and read a draft of the manuscript. Roger Farrington offered his expertise in re-working old photographs. Some of these were supplied by Libby Trott Hills, along with notes and clippings from her mother, Elisabeth Trott's, extensive collections.

The seed for the book was planted by my friend, the noted historic preservationist, Sally Rand. She once asked if I had done a survey of historic buildings at Small Point. I had not, but I promptly did so, identifying some forty-five examples. Most important in my efforts has been the support and technical assistance of my partner Gary Duford, who is better on the computer, to put it mildly.

No doubt, this book will strike some readers as excessive, others as inadequate. Any history is selective; it has to be. So, dear reader, be sure to also read Gloria's two volumes, the Gilmans' *Small Point, "The Cape of Many Islands,"* the *Centennial History of the Small Point Club,* and, for a larger view, Doris Isaacson's *Fair to the Wind.*

Contents

Introduction

Before you read my history, I invite you to consider your own history—the moment of your birth is the beginning of history, your history. Who are you? When and where were you born? Take a piece of paper and write your answer to these questions. You have begun the study of history.

Maybe the thought of studying history just does not appeal to you. The study of history can seem like an endless and useless series of trivia questions: Who was this? When was that? The many facts of history are meaningful and relevant, only when you have a story to tell. Who was president when you were born? In my case, it was Franklin Roosevelt. Going back to your history, when answering "who are you?", you probably mention your parents. Where did they come from? Did you know your grandparents? Think about the places you have known. This is your own history; it is your path.

I now ask you to follow my path through a place called Small Point. You may know it well, or not at all. Follow my path, and as you do so, compare your own path. You might keep that paper handy. Do not forget to save (and label) photographs and other documents of your life.

1

My Background

My parents, Charles and Kathleen Hinkle, first visited Small Point, Maine, in 1931. They found a small, close-knit, firmly established summer community on the coast, made up of Maine families almost entirely, the Manley family of Augusta, and the Sewall family of Bath (the Wright family from Pennsylvania had Augusta connections).

The link was my mother's sister, Constance Peters, known as Polly. Polly was employed by the Small Point Club, a summer hotel and community center founded by Joseph Manley. The club had engaged a Mrs. Higginson from Winnipeg in western Canada to serve as manager. She in turn hired some Canadian girls to work for her; among them was Polly. My mother's family was Canadian; they started out in Boston but fled to Canada at the time of the Revolution.

Polly later enrolled at Massachusetts Institute of Technology, studying architecture and landscape architecture. A classmate was Elizabeth Pattee from Boston, who also had Small Point ties and who had a camp there. Later, they established the firm of Pattee and Peters, Architects and Landscape Architects in Boston. Polly lived with my parents on West Cedar Street on Beacon Hill.

Now we have some ingredients, but we do not know exactly how they fit together. When my parents visited Small Point, the club register shows my father's signature in the summer of 1933, then again in 1934 and 1935, strongly suggesting that my parents stayed there. The register records visitors to the club, not all of whom were actually staying there.[1]

MY AUNT POLLY

Polly enjoyed considerable success as a landscape architect, especially among the wealthy ladies of the north shore of Massachusetts. She particularly enjoyed "bossing a job," as a plan was carried out; she was right there with the crew. Her career was cut short in 1944 when she was stricken with pneumonia. It was wartime; penicillin had been invented but was available only to the military. Eventually, she made a good recovery but suffered circulatory damage that made her susceptible to cold temperatures. She spent several winters in Tucson, where she began a career as tutor to children with learning disabilities.

Polly's role in the lives of me and my sister was like that of a grandmother (we never knew any grandparents). She spent endless time with us, entertaining and teaching us.

In the summer, Polly lived at our camp at Small Point in a primitive guest cabin attached to the garage that for years had no toilet; it did have running water. The Small Point Club closed during the war, and then was run by Barbara Terry, who also served as club president and who moved her family into the club, including three children, Sally, Baldwin, Jr. (Bunny), and baby Grey, along with nursemaid Agnes and a big, black Labrador, Figgy.

In 1944, my parents were elected to club membership, and in 1945, my mother was appointed to the executive committee—a group of strong-minded women like Barbara, Janey Sewall, and Nancy Chandler, who met once a week and closely oversaw the running of the club. In December 1945, the board met in New York and approved the sale of shares in the club to Mr. Charles A. and Mrs. Kathleen Hinkle.

In 1947, Polly succeeded Barbara as manager, a position she held until 1951, aided and restrained by my mother, who had become chairman of the executive committee. Jack Chandler, the family patriarch, was president of the club board; Polly was appalled by his admiration for the Statler Hotels, which she would have considered "common and ordinary!"

When she left the club, Polly was able to purchase from her friend Arthur Sewall the carriage house that had been built for his father, also Arthur Sewall. Around the turn of the century, it was considered desirable to have the horses stabled at a distance from the house and not in an attached barn (as at the nearby home of Joseph Manley). Thus the new carriage house, with five horse stalls, was located at the beginning of what is now Seal Cove Road. The timing turned out to be unfortunate for the automobile had begun to replace the horse and carriage. After a few years, the carriage house was simply abandoned. We children explored it and played there as it was not locked.

Polly kept the first floor intact and transformed the loft into a comfortable apartment where she stayed into early winter, then moved to our house in Brookline where she had an apartment on the third floor.

My parents thought the city unhealthy for children, and the house may have been ill-suited as well, so they looked for a suburban location and found a splendid one in Brookline's "Pill Hill," a neighborhood so popular with physicians that the neighbors' kids sometimes called Dad "Doctor Hinkle."

Aunt Polly sitting on her balcony overlooking the road, surrounded by her plants and holding "Pussycat." (*Photograph, TH*)

Boats, the carriage house that Polly made her home. The boats are later. (*Painting, TH*)

Detail, 1858 atlas map of Sagadahoc County.

DISCOVERY

Let us try to imagine my parents' first trip to the beach at Small Point—on a bright, hot morning at low tide. The scene is breathtaking: acres of hard sand beach, divided by a tidal river that one could easily cross at low tide, beyond the remains of a wrecked schooner, then seemingly endless sand with breaking surf at your right hand, and open ocean beyond. There might have been at most a dozen people partaking of this incredible place.

I have two possible connections between Elizabeth Greenleaf Pattee and Small Point. In the 1880s, there was a Greenleaf Cottage on the beach road, which was destroyed by fire; also, William Pattee was a highly regarded designer of wooden ships, producing the carefully shaped miniature half hulls that became patterns for the actual ships. He designed numerous vessels built in Bath. Pattee is an unusual name. I regret not having more information about Elizabeth, whom I knew well. She was born in 1893 to William G. A. Pattee and Laura Saltonstall, according to *Ancestry.com.*

In 1930, Elizabeth designed for her own use the first part of what was the smallest camp at Small Point. It was one of several camps and cottages built on the rise to the west of the Club Road. The roof of the club was visible from the terrace, along with a glimpse of ocean. The original camp was but a single room, with day beds and a galley kitchen across the rear, and a toilet in a closet. Needless to say, it has been repeatedly altered and enlarged; that original room remains intact.

July, view of Seawall Beach from the Small Point Club veranda. My painting shows the beach as seen from the club, at dead low tide, when the Sprague River could be safely waded across. (*Painting, TH*)

My father, a genial fellow, got to know Harrison Wright, a lawyer from Pennsylvania who had become an Episcopal priest. His wife, Sybil Baldwin, had family connections in Augusta—no doubt, the key to the presence of the Wright family in Small Point. "Mr. Wright," as he was known to practically everyone (never "Harry"), conducted Sunday services at the Small Point Club, the community being nearly all Episcopalian. After the service, Dad would join Mr. Wright in his study (where women were not allowed) for a drink.

The Wrights were not initially cottage owners; for a number of years, they stayed at the club. In September 1929, they bought "Merrymeeting," the large cottage that had been built for the Patten family of Bath.

I remember Mrs. Wright as a small, rather cross lady in a broad straw hat and dark glasses. Camilla Lee told the story of visiting her friend Helen Hoffman, Mrs. Wright's granddaughter, staying up so late that she finally, without permission, stayed the night. The next morning, she appeared with Helen and politely declined to have any breakfast. "Nonsense, Camilla," exclaimed Mrs. Wright, "Sit down and eat your oatmeal!"

Grey Terry provided me with genealogical information about his ancestors and their connection to Augusta, Maine:

> Marie Baldwin Terry, Katherine Baldwin Bliss & Sybil Baldwin Wright were the offspring of Henry Porter Baldwin's second marriage to Sybil Lambard following his first wife's death in 1865. Sybil Lambard was the daughter of Sybil Farnham Lambard of Newburyport and Adam Lambard of Augusta.... [Henry Porter Baldwin served as Governor of Michigan.]
>
> Adam Lambard was an interesting guy. A descendant of Martha Ballard of "A Midwife's Tale," he was described in his obituary as having been for many years "the largest taxpayer in Augusta," having parlayed some land into docks and warehouses, then graduating to distilleries, shipping, etc.—quite the entrepreneur. During the Gold Rush he shipped a disassembled flour mill around the Horn and up the Sacramento River and there made a second fortune selling flour to eager '49ers.

At some point in their post-worship meetings, Mr. Wright told Dad that he ought to build a camp at Small Point. Indeed, he had a lot in the woods, which he would sell at a low price (the year, after all, was 1936). Dad took the offer, and Pattee and Peters had a commission. My parents (who lived in Boston) had but one Maine connection; my father's uncle, Anthony Howard Hinkle, had a cottage at Bar Harbor, which was destroyed in the catastrophic fire of 1947. My father's family spent summers in Osterville, Massachusetts.

The Osterville house overlooked a beach and the ocean The beach was pebbly, not nice, with smooth sand, and to get there one had to cross the Centerville River—by boat. To overcome this impediment, my grandparents applied for and received federal government permission to construct a wooden footbridge with double draw spans controlled by a cable connected to large iron wheels on either side. The bridge was badly damaged in the 1938 hurricane and in subsequent storms; I remember as a small child having to row across and then pick our way through wet salt marsh. I hated that. The bridge was totally removed around 1960.

Osterville, view of the front of my grandmother's house. The rear overlooks Nantucket Sound. The car is my grandmother's red Pierce Arrow. (*Painting, TH*)

My grandmother's reaction to Small Point was a mixture of astonishment and disapproval. Why would her son prefer a simple camp in distant Maine (four hours by motor car from Boston) to her splendid, large house in Osterville, Massachusetts, overlooking a private beach and Nantucket Sound? It was where the whole family could gather during the summer months, and there you have the answer: "the whole family."

After my grandfather's death, my grandmother made alterations to the house, removing the billiards room and converting the library to a music room for my aunt, Jean. Evidently convinced that she could not live year-round in part of the house, Jean later had an incongruous "Cape Cod" style addition constructed at the south end, out of scale with the main house and not even painted the same dark gray. Thus "The Big House" became even bigger.

My uncle, Jim, his wife, and three children soon made themselves at home in "The Big House." Their three children each had their own room, and my family had to choose from various guest rooms. Still, my parents did not abandon Osterville; the camp was, after all, merely a getaway.

The local harbor and yacht club were at Wianno. My uncle Jim who had served in the Navy, was a dedicated sailor who raced his sloop *Fantasy* in the Edgartown Regatta, and had a habit of drafting family members into serving as his crew for weekly races under his command. My Canadian mother called them "our ditsy crew."

The day at Osterville was typically spent at tennis or shopping in the morning, followed by a swim and lunch at the Beach Club, then sailing, then a cocktail party, then dinner—there was always something going on.

Small Point, by contrast, was quiet, private, and simple, which my parents loved. There were two tennis courts, privately owned, and Chase Mellen had come up with a "one design" sailboat for racing; there was a modest nine-hole golf course at Sebasco. There were plenty of cocktails, and above all, that beach. The seeds were planted.

Soon, they made the first addition to the camp, an inexpensively constructed ell with a room and bath for the "maid," what the British would call "the maid of all work." Grandmother, by contrast, had a full staff.

In 1941, a serious remodeling took place, reflecting my parents' decision to have children. The one-story section connecting the main block with the large master bedroom was totally rebuilt after only five years, with two small bedrooms and a bath on the second floor and a dormer to make a bedroom of the attic above the kitchen and dining room. Thus were my sister and I accommodated.

We continued to spend a week at Osterville in June and September, until I was at least nine or ten.

I never knew Mary Freeman Gaff Hinkle, my grandmother, as she died in 1939, the year before I was born. In addition to the splendid cottage on Cape Cod, she had a camp on a pond at Orleans, where she could pursue the hunting of birds. She was evidently a good shot.

Now you are probably wondering, where did the money come from? My great-grandfather, James W. Gaff, came from Scotland and settled on the Ohio River, at Aurora, Indiana, where he operated river steamers, was a banker, and opened both a brewery and a distillery. He knew what people wanted. My grandmother married Charles M. Hinkle, son of a book publishing family that got in on the first mass-published schoolbooks. Unlike his father, who started the business and his older brother, Anthony, who took it over, Charlie was a playboy and a drunk; the marriage produced two sons and a daughter before an amicable separation. He died at the age of fifty-four, at the Homestead in Hot Springs, Virginia, the resort hotel owned by his cousin, Fay Ingalls.

The death of my grandmother, Mary Freeman Hinkle, created a long-lasting family crisis: what to do with "The Big House"? That is a subject for another book. It is tentatively titled *All My Houses,* all about my career in historic preservation.

Portrait of Mary F. Gaff Hinkle, by deLaszlo. (*Coll. TH*)

2

Buildings

OF CAMPS AND COTTAGES

So, now bear with me for a little historic preservation lecture. History can require explanation. As it was intended for seasonal use, Grandmother's house would be called a "cottage." What then is the distinction between a cottage and a camp? It is not a matter of size: a camp can be tiny but it can also be huge.

A camp is a simple structure, generally but not always intended for use in summer. It has no cellar, no masonry wall foundation, and is supported by stone, concrete, or wooden posts. The interior is finished in boards or left with the frame exposed. There is no plaster. The fireplace is the usual source of heat, though stoves are also common. There is no central heat. Water is shut off and drained during the cold months; pipes are exposed under the building.

Camps might be constructed by family members or local handymen. They fairly often display what might be called minimal framing. I visited a camp in the Brightwater neighborhood of Phippsburg that had a roof framed by rough-sawn two-by-threes, 2 feet on center, about 12 feet long. I would not want to have a 300-pound man up there doing roofing—better give the job to a young, thin boy.

A camp can be austere, either because the owners had little to spend on it, or because austerity was a deliberate and essential part of the camp's appeal—a simple life away from the city. Camps of all types and sizes are part of Maine life; we will find a variety of examples at Small Point.

A cottage is essentially a conventional house, set in a seasonal community. Cottages range in size from modest to magnificent; even the grand houses of Newport are referred to as "cottages," and Maine has a goodly share of grand ones too, in Bar Harbor, Islesboro, York Harbor, Kennebunkport, and many other locations. Prominent architects like Peabody and Stearns designed many elegant cottages.

A summer cottage has a cellar and a stone foundation, lots of verandas from which to enjoy the view of the lake or the ocean and may have countless other amenities like pools and stables and tennis courts, reflecting the wealth of the owners. Inside, one finds a variety of wall and ceiling treatments, often with elaborate woodwork, and upper rooms done in plaster.

The Pattee and Peters blueprint is labeled "Camp for Charles Hinkle, Esq." Instead of facing the road, it was oriented toward the Cliff Walk, the rustic path connecting the five buildings on the rise above the Club Road. The driveway and parking were to the rear, but visitors had to walk around the house to reach the front door. So, the front door was seldom used, and everyone came and went through the narrow French doors at the south end (see my painting, *Camp*, below).

The main block contains the large living room and a small dining room. The living room is finished in vertical pine boards stained a pale Prussian Blue. The fireplace is set on a raised hearth, with cabinets on either side and a decorative panel above, curiously, a primitive nativity scene by Massachusetts artist Peter Hunt. The fireplace was a Heatilator, a make popular in the 1930 to 1960 era, which provided a steel firebox, greatly simplifying a mason's task. Now you might think that there is an air space behind the steel sides and back, collecting heat that is released through vents at the front, but it was not so; that would have required a much heavier, cast iron unit. Instead, there are only narrow channels at the front, capturing minimal heat. My friend, Rick Hossman of Royal River Construction, had to take down the chimney to the hearth level in order to remove the remains of the Heatilator. He built a beautiful, real-brick fireplace, which did a better job of heating the huge volume of the high-ceiling living room.

The windows are wooden casements which open in. My mother used to say that with the windows open, "it was just like being outside." That may explain why the house has no screened porch, or veranda of any sort. The windows did not fit tightly, being large

Camp. (*Painting, TH*)

and of wood, and the wind tended to blow them in. In winter, they had to be covered with solid wooden shutters. Interestingly, I now live in Portland in a Tudor-style house with casements, but these are iron and open out, and, with iron frames, they are pretty tight and stormproof.

The small kitchen, later enlarged, was at the north or left end of the main block. The master bedroom was in an ell at the rear, connected by a passage which my mother called "the breezeway," off which were the pantry, a bathroom, and a narrow hallway where the coal-fired water heater was located. A vivid childhood memory is the sound of Mother shaking down the ashes before retiring.

This was indeed a camp, unsuitable for cold weather, but it was not casually under-constructed, like the camp in Brightwater. Pattee and Peters complied with accepted framing rules and lumber sizes, with one exception. With the widespread use of plywood and drywall, it had become standard to work in 48-inch modules with framing spaced 16 inches on center. Given that the camp framing was mostly exposed, it was designed to be symmetrical, evenly spaced between windows and other openings. I nevertheless learned a lot about construction just from living with exposed framing, found everywhere save the living and dining rooms (later covered in the master bedroom, which became our library, equipped with a gas-fired stove for heat).

3

A Summer Place

The whole evolution of summer communities began in the 1860s and 1870s, when cities had become crowded; new industries were appearing, along with huge immigrant populations to man the new factories—nice for the old families who gathered vast profits from making cloth, garments, shoes and such (the Civil War was a tremendous windfall), but at the same time, they beheld their cities losing their charm. So, they discovered the seashore and the lakes to a lesser degree.

Do I dare to write about Small Point? It was supposed to be a secret. Camilla Edge, a Sewall by birth and the wife of the senator as well as the governor of New Jersey, is said to have prevailed upon local and state authorities to post no highway directional signs for Phippsburg, let alone for Small Point. Yet even then, in the 1940s, the Wyman family-owned Head Beach, open to the public, and around 1950, Sumner Sewall opened a popular campground at Hermit Island. So the secret was already out, but still, there were no signs.

Small Point is the southernmost part of the Town of Phippsburg, a 15-mile peninsula having eleven separate villages (each one once having its own school). The Small Point summer community was a world apart; we did not think of ourselves as part of the town of Phippsburg, save for when it came time to pay property tax, or when trying to place a telephone call from away. No telephone operator had ever heard of the place. I remember my mother saying "No, not Fitchburg! No, not Pittsburg! P-h-i-p-p-s-b-u-r-g, Maine!"

Small Point juts into the Atlantic, with a tip of jagged rocks inset with small beaches, the east side looking over the amazing three miles of Seawall Beach, and the west side having a fine large harbor and a long, sheltered inlet called The Branch, which is bounded to the west by Hermit Island. The interior is quiet forests, with a large pond favored in October by my father and his duck hunter friends.

Small Point has one of the most magnificent shorelines on the coast of Maine: high elevations sloping down to marsh or beach divided by the tidal Sprague River, beyond which the long expanse of Seawall Beach extends to the Morse River. Behind the massive, rolling dunes bordering the beach rises Morse's Mountain. The ocean is broken by the three bare ledges known as the Heron Islands, and by Seguin Island, remarkable in its nearly 200 feet of elevation, and the site of Seguin Light, the original tower having been commissioned by George Washington in 1789.

Seguin. (Painting, TH)

One could say that the moon rules Small Point, for every day, twice a day, the magnetic force of the moon causes the level of the ocean to rise and fall. The beach displays hundreds of acres of hard sand at low tide, stretching from the High Rocks to Popham, intersected by Sprague's River below the club and the larger Morse's River, east of Morse Mountain. Both rivers can be forded at low tide, with the right timing, Morse's being known for occasional quicksand created by the strong tidal current.

Then, the tide turns, and gradually, the expanse of beach is swept under the surf until only a stretch of dry sand perhaps 30 feet wide remains along the edge of the beach grass. Sprague's River becomes a churning, treacherous mass of water, dangerous to all but the expert swimmer. If you are caught on the far side, you have two choices: walk a couple of miles over the mountain road or wait.

Before long, the waters start to recede. For those who chose to sit securely on a veranda and take it all in, the scene is dramatic and unfailingly beautiful, further enhanced and varied by the subtle alterations of changing light and weather.

Camilla Sewall Wood furnished me with a partial manuscript of *The Rivers and Marshes of Small Point* by her great-grandmother, Emma Sewall, which was among the papers of Camilla's grandfather, Harold Sewall. Emma Sewall was a gifted writer as well as a noted photographer. Here is her recollection of a visit to the beach and the dunes as a small child. She was born in 1836, so her memories probably go back to around 1846, making this our earliest actual recorded memory:

> Years ago, how many no man knoweth, the Kennebec river had two mouths by which it entered the ocean. It separated at Cox's Head and the peninsula of Sabino, on which the colony of George Popham settled in 1607, must in prehistoric days have been an island. Gradually the western arm of the Kennebec river filled with sand. First a bar covered at high tides; then, as the drifting tree trunks and tangled seaweeds caught on it, after long years it became a salt marsh on the river side while a line of sand dunes fronted the ocean. Among these was an occasional opening, through which in very heavy storms the sea broke and spread its drifting flotage over the marsh.
>
> From the present mouth of the Kennebec river to Small Point it is now a region of sandy salt marshes, traversed by two narrow salt water rivers—Morse's and Sprague's—and divided by Morse's Mountain, formerly called Mt. Ararat, which comes down to the sea itself. It is skirted by fantastic sand dunes, wind-blown and wave-washed, in whose bosoms are buried the drift and wreckage of unknown ages—unwritten history, which in all probability will never be revealed. Outside these marshes and sand dunes extend Popham and Small Point Beaches–the finest and most picturesque on our Coast.
>
> I have often wondered why it is that the inhabitants of the seashore are so much more superstitious than those of the mountains. I suppose it must be from the mystery and uncertainty which always surrounds the sea. I do not think it possible that anything inland could have inspired the awe which as a child I felt in crossing this marsh which has filled in the western arm of the Kennebec.
>
> Imagine, if you can, this place. On one side huge sand drifts and dunes and the thundering of the unseen sea; on the other side—ruin and desolation—the road itself, a zigzag cart path in which our wheels cut deep, and from which the sand fell as they revolved slowly, winding in and out among drift stuff and wreckage of every kind. It is sixty years since I saw it, but I can see it distinctly now. Stumps of giant trees with bleached roots like whitened bones; fragments of masts with rusty irons still attached; the broken stern of a schooner half buried in the sand, its gaping companionway with one door still swinging, showing traces of the light blue paint, which had once adorned it; logs with the owners' marks cut on their sides, their ends rounded by beating on the rocks and rolling in the surf; a piece of a broken windlass; slabs; an old deck bucket, made from a cask, with its frayed rope handle; a broken oar; bits of sheathing; parts of a vessel's frame; dangling strips of black kelp; bushes long ago washed from their native earth; seaweeds and shells,--everything piled in confusion as the drifting high tides from the river or the heavy surf had left it....Over all was a wild cloudy sky and a howling wind.

Emma Sewall's historical and geological theory of the Kennebec River may be open to question, but her childhood memories are distinct and vivid.

Morning Beach. (Painting, TH)

A LITTLE BACKGROUND

What follows is clearly not from my own experience. My path is also my past, leading back into the mists of time. Your path likewise connects with your past. So, we have to rely on the work of historians and on available documents. This is the almost impossible task of history: finding the necessary documents, choosing the "right" ones, and—above all—understanding them. We must be able to visualize the past as it was, not through the lens of the present. Remember, we are standing where someone stood perhaps a century ago, two centuries ago, or even longer.

The mouth of the Kennebec River was the site of the first actual European settlement, but the continent of North America was well-known to Europeans a century before the Popham colony of 1607. We have no memorable date and explorer for the original discovery; there were no doubt many separate discoveries, most of them lost and unrecorded. Here, we are concerned not with discovery, but with exploration and, eventually, settlement.

Small Point was territory of the Wabanaki tribe of native people. No one can say even approximately how long they were there, at least 4,000 years, in some tribal configuration. They had no written language, only oral history, a form that we scarcely understand today though it was standard among early Europeans. The British explorers did not understand their language, nor anything about them. They labeled them dangerous savages.

Vestiges of native occupation are scarce: the occasional burial ground, piles of seashells, and sometimes a tool or arrowhead. They built no permanent structures; they did not excavate the land. They came and went according to the season—Small Point no doubt in warmer months, well inland in winter. They did not invent the wheel. Time had a different meaning.

During my childhood, native people came to Small Point to sell us beautifully made sweetgrass baskets. The aromatic grass was gathered from the salt marshes. That trade disappeared. Native craftsmen have recently revived the making of extraordinary baskets from natural materials.

4

Ancient History

EUROPEAN PRESENCE

In 1524, Verrazano sailed the coast of Maine and mapped it, including Small Point. In 1497, an explorer named Cabot had landed at Newfoundland, and "claimed" the whole continent for England, regardless of having seen but a tiny fragment of it. Sir Humphrey Gilbert, an ardent explorer, noted the presence of fishing vessels from several European countries when he anchored in Small Point Harbor in 1583. In 1603, Martin Pring and George Weymouth kidnapped five Native American men as a sort of circus sideshow and carried them back to England.

There had been tales circulating of great riches to be found for the taking in the New World. The captured native men cleverly took advantage of this somewhat imaginary, exaggerated notion. They learned English and charmed their captors with glowing tales of the treasure awaiting them, if they would kindly return the natives to their home.

No doubt, the appetites of Sir Ferdinando Gorges, Sir John Popham, and their followers were duly whetted. They planned a voyage and a settlement. Gorges was an English aristocrat despite his Portuguese-sounding name, and a man of great wealth, as was Sir John Popham. Together, they founded the Virginia Company.

This was strictly a business venture. By contrast, the Spanish and Portuguese, who colonized South America and did find gold and silver in abundance, saw their ventures as military conquests, defeating the native people and turning the survivors into slaves. The British simply did not anticipate the conflict that they would incite, nor the challenges of coexisting with the native populace.

Anthropologist William Haviland, writing a guest column in *The Working Waterfront*, provides valuable information about the native people of Maine and the Popham colony. One of the captured natives, Skidwarres, sailed as a guide aboard one of Sir George's ships, the *Mary and John*. He guided the two ships to Pemaquid, where the English were introduced to the local chief Tahanedo, who happened to be one of the other four captives, and had also served as a guide to the New World, on a vessel belonging to Martin Pring, one of his captors. Not trusting the English, Skidwarres promptly disappeared into the woods.

The site chosen for the colony was in the district of Chief Sebora, but the grand chief of the Wabenakis in Maine was Bashaba, who lived in the Bangor area. The local chiefs urged Sir George to make a formal visit to Bashaba, but Sir George had little respect for the natives and could not be bothered to make the journey. This bit of arrogance was to set a pattern.

5

The Popham Colony, 1607

The Popham Colony was carefully planned, well-funded, and well-equipped with two vessels carrying tools and supplies including the hardware and fittings for a small ship to be constructed (the two ships that delivered them promptly returned home). That vessel was called the *Virginia*; she was completed in October 1607, ostensibly for local exploration. She had a capacity of 30 tons and a length of 50 feet. The only documentation of the *Virginia* is a sketch in the border of a plan of the fortification known as Fort St. George and the buildings within its walls. Recent archaeology has shown the plan to be remarkably accurate, and that the buildings were in fact constructed as planned. The ship's design was a standard one. A reproduction has been slowly taking shape in Bath.

The plan of Fort St. George, the settlement at Popham, was drawn on site by expedition member John Hunt. Evidence of various structures recently discovered by archaeologists conforms closely to this drawing. The sketch of a sailing vessel at the left is assumed to be the *Virginia.*

There were drawbacks: the colonists, numbering about 100 men, arrived in August and settled on the east side of Cape Small on the Kennebec River near the future site of Civil War-era Fort Popham. Had they chosen the west side, perhaps the wonderfully enclosed harbor known as "The Basin," they would have had better protection from an unusually severe winter.

Captain George Popham, the colony president, died at age seventy-six, leaving Raleigh Gilbert, second in command, as governor of the colony. When spring came, the supply ships returned, bearing an important letter to Gilbert; he had just inherited an estate, probably a manor house, farm lands, and a village or two—a valuable inheritance to say the least. Mr. Gilbert immediately lost interest in the New World, and the settlement was left without an effective leader.

In his excellent history *Coastal Maine,* Roger F. Duncan observes that the native people were "reasonably well disposed toward the colonists," and that the death of George Popham was "almost the only fatality" that occurred during that harsh winter. Duncan is thorough and detailed in his account and clearly at odds with other accounts that state that a number of men died as a result of conflict with the native people. He depends upon the narratives of those who were actually there, but history is full of inconsistencies, and it is said, cynically, that you can prove any historical theory,

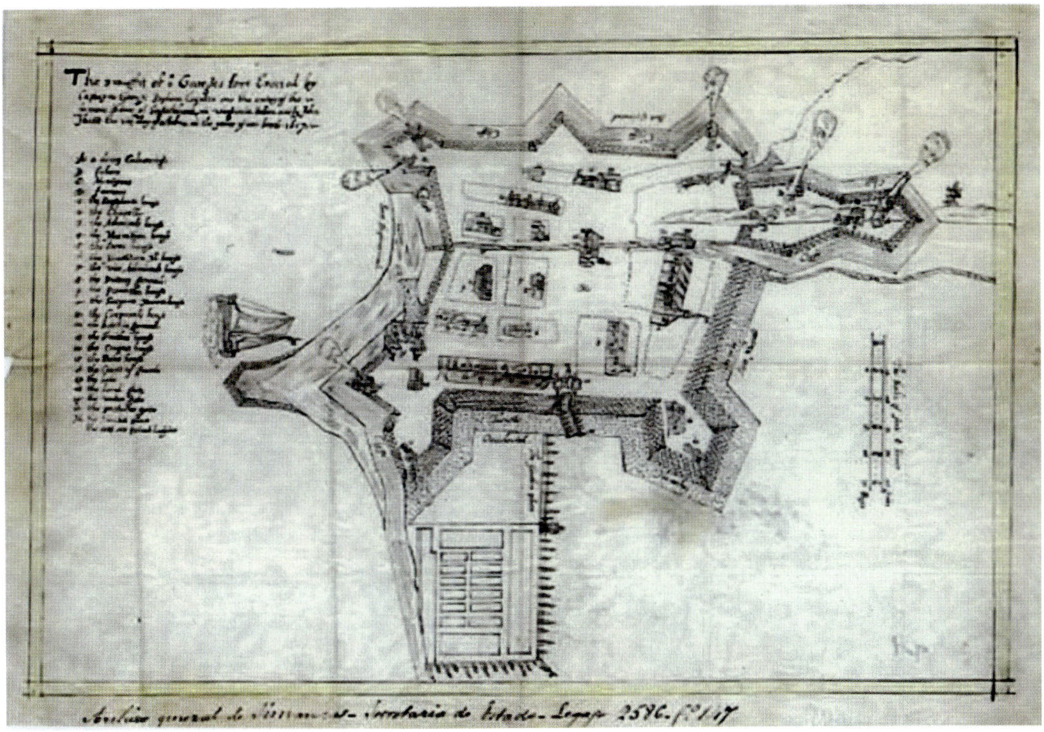

Illustrated plan of Fort St. George. (*Maine Historical Society*)

however far-fetched, with some sort of documentation that is reasonably convincing. So, the colonists boarded the *Mary and John* and their own *Virginia*, returning to England.

There had been no gold or silver. Contrary to the promises of the kidnapped natives, there were no immediate riches to be had. However, the settlers had an abundance of every kind of fish and shellfish, and they were surrounded by endless acres of virgin forest of pine, spruce, oak, and any other species—chestnut was a remarkably useful food and lumber tree before disease wiped it out. These resources were of little use to a group of men with extremely limited means of transporting anything back to England. Thanks to the native people, they were made aware of a major and highly valuable resource: animal pelts. They carried a supply back with them.

The Popham Colony has been labeled "a failure," yet it was not. The settlers assessed the situation and decided to go home, thinking they would gain little by staying. However, they were by no means forced out. Try to imagine being a European explorer in 1607, finding yourself confronted by dense forests, a rocky shore teeming with all manner of fish, a horribly cold winter, and a group of native people dressed in animal skins, speaking an unknown tongue, and potentially dangerous—savages.

The buildings constructed at Fort St. George were basically English country dwellings, timber-framed, and the spaces between the framing members filled with "wattle" or laths made of tree branches, then coated with lime plaster—no match for a harsh

American winter. Heat was from a fireplace or just a hearth with a hole in the roof above for smoke, where the heat was also lost.

Now, think what they were missing, what they had left behind as they dreamed of riches. The settlers came from England. Queen Elizabeth had just ended her glorious reign; her successor, James I, had commissioned an English translation of the Bible that is still a standard edition; and Shakespeare's plays were being produced in the Globe Theatre. In Rome, my favorite artist, Carravaggio, was creating startlingly realistic scenes from the Bible. The English countryside was adorned with extraordinary architecture: great castles and cathedrals, some already dating back a century or more. Also, the nation was looking to expand.

In one sense, this and similar voyages were hoping to be voyages of discovery. The explorers were seeking a passage to "The Indies," eastern Asia. Hence the regrettable assigning of the term "Indians" to the first native people they encountered. The term seems unfortunately permanent, used to this day in government offices, such as the Bureau of Indian Affairs. You will not find it used here.

The presence of the native tribes played an important role in the history of the settlement of Maine. King Charles I never set foot in the "New World;" he looked at the maps provided by Cabot, Captain John Smith, and other explorers and declared that the territory belonged to England. The French king was doing likewise. In 1622, Charles chartered the "Province of Maine," consisting of the territory between the Merrimack and Kennebec Rivers. In 1629, this was amended to start at the Piscataqua River. The "patent" was held by Sir Ferdinando Gorges, who set the capital, called Gorgeana, on the York River, just north of the present Maine Turnpike bridge (the site is now wooded; there is nothing to see). The town, now York, evolved slowly, beset by conflict with native people and faced with the grueling tasks of creating farms out of wilderness. In 1694, a native invasion captured a sizable number of inhabitants and burned many houses, and this was in the more established southern corner. In Georgetown, very little was happening.

Meanwhile, life in England was increasingly chaotic, with parliament determined to defeat King Charles I, which they eventually did, executing him in 1749. That miserable tale is beyond the scope of this history.

Still, a series of "proprietors" gained title to large segments of what is now Phippsburg and tried to interest prospective settlers. "Gained title" requires some consideration. The native people had no concept of "title," that is, legal ownership of parcels of land with certain rights included. So, when the settlers offered token payment for tracts of land, the native leaders (no doubt amused at the whole absurdity of it) agreed and executed the deeds. Then came orders to clear out. The tribes fought back, but they were gradually shoved out of their territories, which they had held for centuries.

I am often asked about "Royal Grants." The notion is that the British crown actually gave parcels of land to individuals. This was not the case. The various monarchs were not directly involved in the New World settlement, leaving those tasks to wealthy investors known as proprietors, whom we would call "developers." The cost of getting to the new colonies was only the beginning; the land had to be surveyed (by George Washington and others), then actively promoted to potential settlers. This was all business. Along the way, settlers did, as a sort of formality, occasionally purchase land from native owners—a detail entirely ignored by the British authorities.

One of the major forces contributing to the ultimate defeat of the native people was their lack of resistance to European diseases, such as cholera, yellow fever, whooping cough, and tuberculosis. Some tribes lost 90 percent of their populations to European diseases. Those who survived were forced to live on reservations, but that is a later story.

The English were not alone in claiming portions of the New World. Samuel de Champlain explored the Maine coast and produced remarkably accurate maps. The French claimed title to Acadia (as they called the Maine coast) and established settlements that were brutally destroyed by English forces under the leadership of Captain Samuel Argal. The French were welcomed by the native people; even the Jesuits, famously controversial, made many native converts. The native people worked closely with the French settlers in trapping animals for fur. The French retreated to the north and west and emerged to fight a war decades later.

6

Fort Augusta, 1714

The British kept on trying. In 1714, a group of capitalists called the Pejepscot Proprietors laid out a substantial farming village with a fortification on Small Point Harbor near the present-day Baily's Beach. Dr. Oliver Noyes served as director and was a major investor. The stone fort was named Fort Augusta. An east–west road was laid out connecting the settlement to the Kennebec (Emma Sewall in *The Rivers and Marshes of Small Point* writes of trying to retrace this pathway). Other roads were planned to link a number of large farms.

The Fort Augusta settlement came to a hasty end when it was attacked by native warriors with flaming arrows (their version of rockets). The settlers could not fight the fires since their well was outside the walls of the fort; they jumped into their boats and headed south, never to return. A common complaint that surfaced here was that the English military failed to provide for the active defense of outlying settlements. The military had more places to protect than they could cover.

Curiously, you cannot visit the remains of Fort Augusta; there just are not any left. The stones of the fort may well have been salvaged much later for foundations. A modern cottage is said to occupy the approximate site. An article in the *Bath Enterprise* in 1898 reported on the amateur excavation of the foundation of the fort, revealing a stone base laid in mortar and topped with a brick wall, also mortared. This should have been a red flag: the presence of bricks and mortar would indicate a structure considerably later than 1714. There were brickyards in Phippsburg by 1790.

The Augusta settlement was, in any case, a major undertaking, suddenly canceled. Permanent settlement was still many years away. This pattern of conflict between native people and European settlers effectively delayed the establishment of the new colonies. In *The Eastern Frontier*, Charles Clark states that "York, Kittery and Wells were the only settlements in Maine that remained inhabited at all throughout the period from 1689 to the Peace of Utrecht in 1713." Clark further describes the conflict:

> The nature of Indian warfare, with its swift, silent attacks, its ambuscades, its disregard of age and sex, and its deliberate cruelties, must have promoted a special hatred of the natives—matched only, perhaps, by the growing resentment of the red men themselves over the clearly unjust and ceaseless encroachment on their hunting grounds and way of life by people who, unlike the French, displayed little interest in their welfare. Imagine the reaction of Captain Convers and his fifteen men at Wells ... forced ... to watch helplessly

> from their garrison house while a band of Indians disposed hideously of an English prisoner.... the savages first stripped Diamond, then castrated him, sliced between his fingers and toes, covered his body with gashes into which they thrust firebrands.[1]

A powerful incentive for prospective settlers in the New World was the actual, legal ownership of a tract of land. Farmers in England were tenants on land owned by a lord. John Smith is quoted in *Maine Coast*:

> Here there are no hated Landlords to racke us with huge rents.... no tedious pleas in law with their many years disputations for Justice.... Here every man may be master and owner of his owne labour and land.[2]

Of course, there was a drawback; most of the new land had never before been extensively cultivated. The lands were generally well-forested, and the soil laden with stones. The colonists had to start from scratch.

Given that Fort Augusta was to be a farming community, you may wonder what they intended to raise. The notion that Maine has no good farmland is ridiculous; there are good fields in Small Point, some now abandoned to forest or new highways, some still visible. Let us review some basic crops and farm animals.

Cattle: Cows need hay. Small Point provided a bonanza of healthy, ready-to-harvest hay that needed no cultivation, only a scythe. This was salt marsh hay, hundreds of acres of which grew in the marshes of the Sprague and Morse Rivers. Earliest maps show the land owned in separate plots by local farmers.

Sheep: Until well into the nineteenth century, wool was the fiber for all clothing—summer and winter. Linen was a minor crop that was hard to prepare, and cotton, not

Photograph by Emma Sewall, "Sharpening the Scythe." (*From* Message Through Time, *by permission of Abbie Sewall, author*)

grown in Maine, was encumbered with seeds. Maine farmers had thousands of sheep. They grazed happily on rough ground.

Corn: A standard crop that did require plowing, sowing, and cultivating, corn served as animal feed and was ground into meal. The native people did cultivate it.

Fruit: Apples grew well in the rocky soil and were planted in large orchards, some of which endured for decades, even centuries. Wild fruits included raspberries, blackberries, and blueberries. These are but a small sampling of the products of farms in Small Point and throughout Maine.

Small Point was a farming community. The fishing industry was limited to the west side including Hermit Island, whereas the villages of West Point and Sebasco, to the north and west were mostly the homes of fishermen. By around 1750, the native threat had subsided, and families had begun to settle, this time permanently. Nearly all of them had been already established in towns of greater security, as opposed to being newcomers from Europe. America was always the land of promise, and people were nearly always ready to try a new location.

Those who chose Small Point seemed satisfied; they stayed for generations. The Wyman family came from Yarmouth and settled around 1750 at Parker's Head, northeast of Small Point. The 1857 atlas map shows a number of Wyman houses.

A 1752 map shows a McIntyre on Hermit Island, and also a Wallace. These were both fishing families, and historian Christopher Sewall speculates that they may have been coming to Small Point Harbor to fish for generations. It is hard to pin down just who was the original settler of Small Point; we know that in 1767, Nathaniel Sylvester was building his remarkable house. Isaiah Wyman in 1793 purchased a large tract including the south end of the Point. The Wymans constructed a log cabin on the Back Bay—the quickest solution for shelter that does not call for sawn lumber. A family cemetery remains near that site. On a nearby hilltop, they built a timber-framed house, which, with additions, sheltered the family for seven generations and remains in the family as of 2015. The two-story house visible from the main road probably dates from about 1820—a substantial dwelling with a chimney at each end and a central hallway. Located like an ell behind it is the earlier structure, which appears to be a hall-and-parlor example, built for Isaiah Wyman.

Nathaniel Sylvester's cape is the earliest surviving house in Small Point, or in Phippsburg. It is a large, central chimney cape whose five-bay front is notable for narrow, four-over-four windows. These window openings are unique in my experience and are unquestionably original. The four-over-four sash layout is clearly a later replacement. The common glass size was 7 × 9 inches, and most early houses in rural Maine had nine-over-six window layouts. I was able to restore the windows of the Fletcher House using old salvaged sash from as far away as Exeter, New Hampshire, that fit the openings nicely, or with a little planing. Thanks to Gloria Gray, whose *Small Point, Volume I* contains what must be the earliest known photograph of the Sylvester House I have the answer to my question: the original layout of the sash was nine-over-nine lights, glass size being 7 × 9 inches—most unusual.

It is the interior which makes the Sylvester House, "one of the most important houses in Maine," to quote restoration expert Les Fossel. The house is still standing, and we can only hope that it receives the care that it deserves.

Photograph showing the oldest portion of the Isaiah Wyman House. (*TH*)

Photograph of the left side of Sylvester House. (*From* Small Point, Volume I *by Gloria Grey, by permission of the author*)

Photograph of the exterior of Sylvester House. (*TH*)

Photograph of the left parlor. (*TH*)

Photograph of the right parlor. (*TH*)

The two front parlors are finished in high Georgian style. The right parlor has a fully paneled fireplace wall, the fireplace being flanked by wide, fluted pilasters. There is a corner cupboard, also framed by fluted pilasters fitted with a glazed door with arched top and an arched, raised panel below. In the left parlor is a slightly different corner cupboard with pilasters; here, the top has a carved shell arch and three shaped shelves over a door with two vertical panels. The fluting of the cupboard pilasters extends the full length, whereas those of the fireplace have stopped fluting. The window openings are doubtless original, though the sash has been changed to four-over-four. The house remains largely intact, having typically lost its chimney years ago in favor of indoor plumbing. Replacement of the central chimney would be fairly straightforward as the three fireplace openings survive.

The remarkable survival of the Sylvester House is owed to its possession in the family until 2005. The location, in what was the village of Small Point, made it a natural choice for the first school, and when a schoolhouse was built around 1840, it was located just down the lane, on the main road. A store and post office, owned by the Sylvesters, was located across the road. The teacher at the Small Point School at the time of its closing in 1958 was Marguerite Sylvester Blair. Her husband, Winthrop Blair, was versed in all the building trades, and my parents were fortunate to have him as caretaker of the camp after the death of Swanton Wyman.

Retired from teaching, Marguerite Blair opened a laundry and gift shop in the house. I remember accompanying my father when he dropped off and collected laundry, but I never saw the parlors, and I would not have appreciated them anyway, way back in the 1950s.

7

The Village Center

The Gilmans' history refers to the dam across the inlet by the old Sylvester store. Richard R. Lowell is said to have built the dam with a lease from Ellis Sylvester, owner of the site. The mill was probably used to grind grain; it did not last long. There is also a fascinating reference to "James R. Lowell's store, which set across from the Sylvester store, at the foot of schoolhouse hill." I know of no other mention of Lowell's store, nor any photograph, but the 1858 atlas identifies its owners as "J. E. Lowell" at the Fletcher House and "store" next to it. There is no Sylvester store shown across the road; the "store and PO" are at the town landing. It would appear that the store and post office by the Aliquippa and the town landing were relocated after 1858 to the Sylvester house on the main road, now the home of the Gilliam family. Still later, around 1900, a Small Point Beach Post Office was opened at Wyman's store, serving the summer community. A strictly seasonal operation, it had the enviable zip code of 04567. Of the many local post offices, the only remaining branch is at Sebasco Estates. The main post office is a 10-mile drive from Small Point. No ice cream for sale.

The 1858 map is a source of information, but there are errors: Sylvester is "Solister" and Totman is "Tolman."

There are three houses at the north end of Hermit Island, identified as Kendall, Johnson, and W. Morse. A "J. Sprague" house is shown near the entrance to the present Sumner Lane (lilac bushes), but no Manson cottage or tavern is shown. The Bodwell Grange had yet to be built. There was quite a neighborhood on the Back Bay where the Lobster House stands—houses owned by W. Sprague, J. Wallace, and X. Day. One of these became the *c.* 1830 Thompson House. Two other Sprague houses are nearby, as was Abner Lowell's.

The Daniel Blaisdell house is labeled "T. Rowe;" a Ruel W. Rowe is listed in the town memorial records as having served in the Civil War. It is unknown if this was his son, or whether he was the owner prior to Thomas Pye.

There is a Fletcher, to the north of Rowe's. In Popham, the map shows only one hotel, the Dehamda House, the name perhaps a combination of the three names. The Aliquippa Hotel is shown, along with the Lowell "Square House."

Identified as "SH," the Small Point schoolhouse was a typical wooden building with gable to the front and two doors. I remember children playing at recess. In 1958, the consolidated elementary school opened. School buses were the new regime. The old

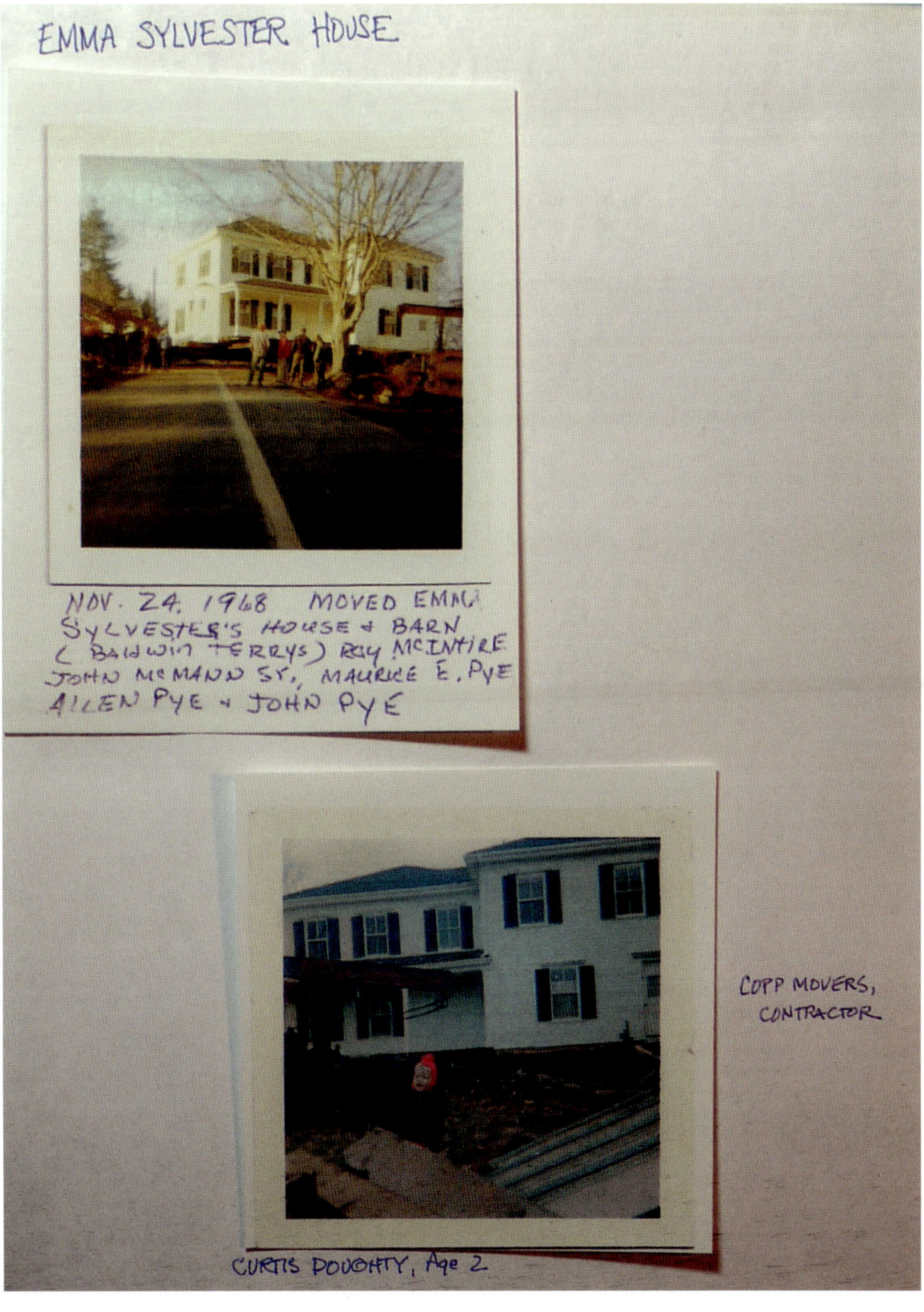

Scrapbook page: Moving the Emma Sylvester house. (*Courtesy of Carol Doughty*)

school stood vacant and neglected, and ultimately a heavy snow collapsed the roof. It would have been fairly easy to preserve, but no one bothered. There may even have been a certain contempt for what had become obsolete, yet the school at Parker's Head has been carefully preserved.

With time, the former village center lost its identity. The Sylvester store became a private residence, its barn removed. The Lowell store vanished without a trace. The Emma Sylvester House was moved across Main Road to a more private site on Sprague Road; a sole apple tree marks the old site.

Another Sylvester house became the residence of Houghton Trott. It survives, including a large, newer, carriage barn. Carol Doughty tells me that the house was, for a time, the Small Point schoolhouse.

The Blairs had a son, Maurice, who became a local building contractor, and a somewhat controversial one. Maurice did not always follow his client's instructions. I persuaded my mother to hire him to build her new guest cottage, but he failed to correctly execute her careful design for mirrors (from an English hotel), so she fired him. His replacement, "Scotchy" Doyle, finished the guest cottage. Later, he built a raised deck at Billy Hoffman's guest house which during a big cocktail party separated from the house and crashed some 15 feet to the ground, causing serious injuries. "Scotchy" disappeared.

Maurice eventually moved to Florida and the Sylvester Homestead, including some 40 acres extending back to the marsh, was sold at auction to a young member of the St. John family. What was once substantial farmland acreage extends to the east and abuts the Morse Mountain Preserve, appropriately.

8

The Revolutionary War

When studying history, it is never possible to simply move chronologically, though this may seem a logical way to go. As you follow your path, others are following theirs at the same time. So now, having followed the Sylvesters until their departure in 2005, we drop back to the 1770s and the Revolution. Small Point was just being settled. Nathaniel Sylvester was building his wonderful house.

Small Point, Morse's Mountain, and Seguin Island make a bold presence at the mouth of the Kennebec. Yet these were never military targets; there simply were not enough concentrated buildings to justify an attack. Bath was safely "up river." The nearest coastal conflict was at Falmouth, where, on 17 October 1775, Captain Henry Mowat laid waste to the town. Citizens were shocked; they had come to accept Mowat as a British officer who meant them no harm. When they recognized his ship, they assumed that he had come to purchase food and supplies.

Mowat gave them two hours to get out of town. He was under orders from his admiral. Most of the town's residences and public buildings were burned. It should be noted that, just as Phippsburg was originally part of Georgetown, so Portland was later separated from Falmouth. Mowat's attack is often referred to as the burning of Portland. It was an enormous incentive to the colonial armies.

The Revolutionary War was scarcely a traditional war with two trained armies facing off in major battles on land. Instead, there were repeated encounters by small forces on land, but mainly between ships at sea. The British concluded early on that they could not successfully defeat the American forces on land, so their plan was to effectively starve them and destroy their commerce by blockading the coast. In a real sense, this was a war about trade. America had become a valuable source of lumber and other raw materials, trading with British possessions in the Caribbean and with Britain herself. From about 1774 to 1814, this commerce was fraught with attacks, confrontations, capture of ships and cargoes, death, and destruction.

The British were at one huge disadvantage: it took a vessel from five to ten weeks to reach the Maine Coast, and then the officers and crew had to find sources of food and water, never mind other provisions. Also, the coast of Maine offered so many places for the enemy to hide that British ships found blockading any river or harbor impossible, and their warships were large and slow. The colonists made use of all manner of small sailing vessels capable of rapid maneuvers.

Men from Phippsburg hastened to join the local militias (hence the Second Amendment), traveling to join the conflict. Daniel Blaisdell's name appears on a list of men entitled to benefits for their service. He does not appear on the town's memorial plaque, which lists Small Point residents Stephen Lowell, Daniel Morse, Jonathan Morse, Nathaniel Sprague, Nathaniel Sylvester, Nathaniel Wyman, and William Wyman, as well as others, some of whom may have come from Small Point, and which may have other omissions.

Cornwallis's surrender to General Washington at Yorktown in 1781 and the subsequent Treaty of Paris in 1783 marked the end of the war and the establishment of the United States of America. However, the conflict was far from over. Britain imposed a series of trade restrictions (which were cleverly circumvented). Privateers often became pirates, brutally seizing cargo ships and murdering their crews. Yet in Maine and along the New England coast, ship-building revived and flourished, and a well-equipped navy took shape, including the *United States* and the *Constitution*, the latter carefully preserved in Boston Harbor.

The British were little better than the pirates, capturing American vessels and seizing the crew for their own use. Thomas Jefferson's response was to impose a total embargo: no American ships were to sail to foreign ports. It was at this time that the first fort at Popham was built, to enforce the embargo and to keep in our ships, not to keep out an enemy.

The so-called War of 1812 continued the hostilities between Britain and the United States, while achieving little. The most famous encounter—between the British *Boxer* and the American *Enterprise*—resulted in the death of both captains. Both were buried on Munjoy Hill, and it was said that the battle was visible from the newly constructed watchtower on the hill, which survives and is operated as a museum by Greater Portland Landmarks.

It is not the purpose of this particular local history to thoroughly explore the convolutions of the Revolution and the War of 1812. As the century progressed, world trade flourished. In the 1840s, there were seven rum distilleries in Portland, along with J. B. Brown's massive sugar refinery. According to Duncan (whose history of the wars is exemplary), "In 1860 Maine distilled 452,000 gallons of rum, most of it in Portland." We will return to this stimulating subject in a later chapter.

MEN AT SEA

America was settled for commerce. Trade was almost entirely dependent upon maritime shipping, whether for short distances or back and forth to Europe. Bath was (and still is) a major ship-building city, and wooden vessels were built at Phippsburg along the Kennebec. Ships had to be manned.

Now, going to sea had a certain appeal—an excitement and challenge. Young men signed on, some as young as twelve or even ten, and they found a mixed blessing or outright hell. The famous landscape architect Frederick Law Olmstead could not decide what to pursue as a young fellow, so he signed on to a ship captained by a family friend. The profession of landscape architect did not exist in 1910.

Once at sea, Olmstead suffered such extreme seasickness that he was unable to work at all. Later he contracted cholera and other diseases common to the trade, narrowly escaping serious injury. His shipmates were a crude and sometimes abusive lot, kept in line by the constant threat of corporal punishment. Men were lost during foul weather or while setting sails up the tall masts, others deserted, replacements had to be found. In the early eighteenth century, British crews often included sailors captured from American ships.

Olmstead's is a typical story. A seaman's life was seldom pleasant, to put it mildly. The romance of going to sea still had some voltage, but it tended to flicker. Fifteen years was considered a good span for a wooden vessel. Many met their ends sooner—in violent storms; grounding on shoals, particularly along the east coast of Cape Cod; fire, especially onboard coal or lime carriers; and collisions. Some vessels just disappeared without a trace and were never found. Sometimes, bodies washed up on the shore; often, they never reappeared.

9

The Lowells Come to Small Point

According to Doris Isaacson, the author of *Fair to the Wind*, Stephen Lowell was the first of that famous Massachusetts family to venture into Maine, seeking timber for ships' masts. Mrs. Isaacson did extensive research for her history of Phippsburg, and it remains a most useful reference. In 1797, John Lowell purchased a large tract on the harbor from John Tyng. Within a few years, the Lowell family became a major presence in the Small Point section of Phippsburg. The atlas map of 1858 shows eleven Lowells along the main road near the harbor.

The Lowells of the eighteenth century and into the nineteenth were mainly involved in shipping; a list of Lowell shipmasters is truly impressive. One of these, Abner Lowell, having prospered as a captain, decided to retire to a quieter life on the coast of Maine. Probably in his thirties, Abner Lowell chose Phippsburg where his family had already settled.

John Lowell had built the first conventional, timber-framed house in the immediate neighborhood in about 1790. Sawn lumber for the house may have come from the first Morse sawmill, which was located on North Creek. It became known as the "Square House" and was home to several generations of Lowell families.

Captain Abner met Nancy, daughter of Isaiah Wyman, and asked her to marry him, which she did. So delighted was Isaiah that he presented his son-in-law with a huge tract of land comprising the east side of Small Point and containing some 300 acres, land suitable for sheep pasture, with some good fields. Lowell chose for his home a site by the road on a prominent rise. The tidal Back Bay was visible behind the house, and for decades, it provided a way to deliver building materials by barge to a stone jetty. However, retired seamen were not eager to gaze at the sea. Parker's Head village, for example, was home to both active and retired men of the sea, and their houses all face the road and are grouped tightly together, the antithesis of life on the water.

The Abner Lowell House, built in 1835, is a large, Late Federal-style cape with two chimneys and a central hallway and stairs. An ell extends to the left, containing the kitchen and related spaces. Two barns were built, on each side of the road. A small barn at the left end appears to pre-date the house. In front of the house stood a huge linden tree, said to have been transported from England and planted by Captain Lowell (seems unlikely, but linden is not a native species). This house has played an essential role in the history of Small Point and survives largely intact, with additions as noted.

Postcard view of the Lowell "Square House."

The Linden Tree, the Abner Lowell/Percy House. (*Painting, TH*)

You may question my "Federal" label for the main block, and 1835 is indeed late for the style. However, people built what they wanted, or what their builder thought should be built, so there are plenty of late or transitional examples in the strong-minded state of Maine.

Tallman B. Lowell, son of John, built Lowell's Hotel in 1836, one of America's earliest hotels and a successful venture for nearly a century. A large two-and-a-half-story structure, the hotel was somewhat in the Federal style, with nine-over-six window sash. Various additions were made over the years, creating a total of 20,000 square feet. The hotel was operated as a resort, with steamer service provided via the New Meadows River as well as from Portland. It was later named the Aliquippa Hotel, after a native princess. Some specific connection between the princess and Small Point is missing; it is more likely that Tallman Lowell just liked the name.

Tallman was known as "Squire Lowell;" he was the head of the family and the local entrepreneur. Among many achievements, the squire was responsible for damming the salt marsh northeast of the road to create an ice pond. There was even a conveyer of sorts to transport the ice to the town landing.

It is likely that the Fletcher House of 1790 and the Webber House, a somewhat later cape, were both moved to this neighborhood, under Lowell's supervision, from a location on Morse's Mountain. I have found no documentation showing the year of the relocations. The Fletcher House comes to play an important role in my history; the Webber House stands vacant, resulting in occasional hints to me from friends. I am told, by Susan St. John, that the old foundations of both houses may still be seen on a lane off the Morse's Mountain Road. A pilgrimage has yet to be made.

Was Abner Lowell duly impressed by the magnificent stretch of coastline that his father-in-law had given him? Probably not, for in 1830, it had no exceptional value. It was at best sheep pasture. Small Point was a largely self-sufficient community of farms. The retired captain evidently liked his farm as he spent the rest of his days there. However, his son Abner craved a more challenging life and in 1850 moved to California, where the action was. The rest of the family evidently lost interest in Small Point and headed to California or somewhere in between. The Aliquippa Hotel was sold in 1887 to Samuel Sylvester. The huge Abner Lowell parcel was available.

10

Enter Joseph Bodwell

Every phase of history depends upon an individual—a person with goals and dreams who inspires others. History does not just happen, nor is it the result of trends or eras. Look for the person who started it all. Small Point was transformed by Isaiah Wyman, the first European settler, to a lesser degree by Abner Lowell, and to a much greater degree by Joseph Bodwell, the new owner of the Abner Lowell holdings. He made the initial purchase in 1883.

THE SUMMER COMMUNITY

The evolution of the summer communities began in the 1860s and 1870s. Cities were losing their charm, becoming noisy and smoky. Coal had begun to replace hydropower for factories and was in increasing demand by railroads, creating new industries in mining and shipping, Maine partaking of the latter. Those handsome four- and five-masted schooners, many built by Bath yards, were nearly all used to haul thousands of tons of coal from the mining states to New England—so much for the romance of sailing. Wind power was used to drive the huge vessels because engines would have taken valuable cargo space and consumed coal.

People of even modest means were discovering the seashore, and, to a lesser degree, the lakes. They wanted to get away from coal, smoke, and immigrant workers.

Smart entrepreneurs responded to the new fashion, hastily erecting large hotels along the New England shore where folks from the city might partake of the healthy sea air and dine on nourishing shore dinners. Small Point escaped the big hotel era; it was not sufficiently accessible. The sole hotel, Lowell's Hotel on the harbor, predated the late nineteenth-century resort era, though it was a resort hotel. Popham Beach boasted two large hotels, the Rockaway and the Riverside, as well as several smaller inns. You could get to Popham by regular steamer from Bath or Portland. As it was accessible, Popham became a booming resort community.

The remains of the steamer dock were present on the shore of the Kennebec River as of 2017 but were due to be removed by a neighbor who found them unsightly. Townspeople and the Board of Selectmen strenuously objected to no avail.

Most of Maine's large hotels, being of wood-frame construction and located in small towns or villages, were eventually destroyed by fire. There was no way to stop a hotel fire. Within ten minutes, a small blaze would have the whole structure involved. Sprinkler systems—the only means of controlling a small fire in a big wooden building—were yet to be invented and would not work in winter in a closed hotel. Some of the grand old-timers do survive: the Claremont on Mount Desert Island; Wentworth-by-the Sea in New Castle, New Hampshire; and a piece of the Lookout in Ogunquit, to name a few fairly local examples.

Yet the fashion was ever-changing. In the 1880s, families began having their own summer houses, often grouped in summer communities. Ambitious developers jumped on that new fashion, envisioning dozens of these communities, often consisting of hundreds of building lots. Among them was Joseph R. Bodwell. Small Point was to be transformed.

In 1883, Joseph Bodwell and Melville Spinney took possession of the Abner Lowell holdings, formerly owned by Isaiah Wyman; the Wymans remained to the west and north, and the Boston Gunning Club owned the southern end of the point.

Joseph Bodwell's story sounds like the "typical" American success story, though relatively few Americans actually succeeded at this rate or to this height. Born to a poor farming family in Methuen, Massachusetts, the part of that town which later became the city of Lawrence, he took a job working on construction along the Merrimac River in Lawrence. The work required large amounts of quarried stone. Bodwell saw an opportunity in the quarrying and transportation of stone and started his own company. Somehow, he got to further his career on Vinalhaven Island, where granite was good and plentiful. Also, the demand was high. An even better grade and color of granite was to be found on the mainland, at Hallowell, and Bodwell shifted his operations and soon became the president of one of the largest granite suppliers in America, sending stone to Washington, Philadelphia, Erie, Atlanta, Chicago, St. Louis, Milwaukee, Indianapolis, New York, Boston, Buffalo, and many other cities, chiefly for use in government buildings, but also for the towers of the Brooklyn Bridge. In the District of Columbia, his granite was used to construct what is now the Executive Office Building.

Writing in *The Island Journal*, historian Harry Gratwick states that the success of the granite industry brought almost 3,000 new residents to Vinalhaven by 1900. Like Carnegie and other tycoons of Bodwell's day, Bodwell paid his workers as little as possible; in the 1870s, according to Gratwick, a man earned $1.50 for "a brutal 10-hour day."

The Bodwell Company continued after Bodwell's death, and in 1899, it had its most famous and challenging order: eight huge 55-foot columns for the new Cathedral of Saint John the Divine in New York City. They were produced in two sections and transported by barge to a Hudson River wharf. Then, they were loaded onto special trucks and moved down Amsterdam Avenue. It took nineteen days for the first batch to make the land trip; after that, the process was somewhat accelerated.

Joseph Bodwell's business interests changed and broadened in the 1880s, when, amply provided with capital, he ventured into real estate development. He was also involved in politics; he was twice elected mayor of Hallowell, and, being highly popular, was elected governor of Maine in 1886—the same year that he and Spinney began the project known as "Cliffstone."

The Bodwells lived in an impressive Italianate mansion in Hallowell—ironically, a wooden building (granite was, admittedly, used mainly for government and institutional structures). After years of neglect, it has been appropriately restored including a period color scheme, and he was the initial owner of the first summer cottage at Small Point, also extant (with alterations).

I came along well after Joseph Bodwell and his successor at the cottage, Colonel Watson, yet the house is full of memories for me: from the days of Chase and Sarah Mellen and their children, Chase and Abigail, to the present owner, Elena Vandervoort and her late husband, Peter—what an interesting group. The Mellens will appear in this book as founders of the Summer School (my first job) and the Vandervoorts and I were closely involved in the Small Point Club. All of this led to many a happy evening, as well as serious conversation, at the Bodwell Cottage (which was called "Sea Winnocks").

Joseph Bodwell was married twice: his first wife, Eunelee Fox, died in 1857, without issue; Bodwell then married her sister, Hannah C. Fox, by whom he had a daughter, Persis, and a son, Joseph Fox Bodwell, born in 1862.

Joseph Bodwell's legacy also survives in the Charles Paine Cottage, built in 1907 on the rise behind the club. Charles Paine was the son of Jotham Paine and Persis Mary Bodwell, Joseph Bodwell's only daughter. Charles leased the cottage as a year-round residence to Mrs. Arnold, an artist described as a recluse (perhaps explaining why she chose to live at Small Point, alone, through long winters). She designed the large stone bas-relief over the fireplace on the face of the massive stone chimney. Albert Thompson and his sons stoked and cared for the furnace. In the late 1940s, Charles Paine sold the cottage to Camilla Edge, who gave it to her daughter, Camilla Edge Lee.

Photograph of the Charles Paine/Lee Cottage. (*TH*)

Though he appeared to be a man of rugged health, Bodwell suffered a series of heart attacks while serving as governor, in 1887. He appeared to recover, but a final one abruptly ended his life. His lying in state at the capitol and the huge funeral procession were emblematic of Victorian mourning.

"CLIFFSTONE"

If Abner Lowell failed to appreciate what he had, Joseph Bodwell was fully aware that he had in his possession one of the greatest and most dramatic parcels on the coast of Maine. His engineer laid out a summer cottage community of some two hundred lots connected by a system of roads.

Just when the four main roads of "Cliffstone" were built is not fully documented. Most of the connecting roads were never constructed. The only road in place prior to the development was what is now Sumner Lane, leading south from the main road to the beach by Sprague River, providing access to the beach for local residents and fishermen. One early house stands by this road, known as the Manson Cottage, by local legend, said to have been an inn and tavern. There were several early houses in this area, now gone but marked by lilac bushes, and near the beach stood two summer cottages, owned by Dr. Anderson and a family named Greenleaf, both of which burned.

The Manson Cottage was acquired by Governor Sumner Sewall and heavily remodeled, the entire interior of the old cape section made into a single room. Evidence of a 1790s structure is at best slight. *The Industrial Journal* published the following, dated July 25, 1884:

> At great labor and expense a romantic road has been constructed from Small Point Harbor wharf to the southern bluff, and upon the smaller beach. One marsh covered with water to a depth of four feet has been filled in. On the high land just to the east of the new road to the beach is the site selected for Mr. Bodwell's cottage, on which work will be commenced this fall.... Farther south, on a commanding height, is the proposed site for the large hotel.

The Industrial Journal is often inaccurate, relying on second-hand information from developers and contractors. Reference to the "southern bluff" and to the filled marsh are vague or unlikely; none of the "Cliffstone" roads traversed a marsh. Two cottages were built within the following three years, owned by Bodwell and his Augusta friend, Joseph Manley. Bodwell's was completed in 1886, a year before his death, and Manley's in 1888. The "romantic road" joined the first road near the beach. A third road, the Club Road, was not built until 1890, to the west of the Bodwell and Manley cottages, which were sited on elevated ground with panoramic views of the beach and ocean, now largely blocked by trees.

Joseph H. Manley of Augusta was a patriarch of the summer community. His family being larger than Bodwell's, he established the Manleys as Small Point's leading clan, until the Sewalls came along.

Joseph Manley married into an even more important Augusta family; Susan Hannah Cony was the daughter of Samuel Cony, who served as governor of Maine during the

Two early views of the Anderson Cottage. (*photographs, Trott coll. LH*)

Portrait of Joseph Manley. (*Wikipedia*)

Civil War, and Mercy H. Sewall Cony. Thus two important Maine families, the Sewalls and the Conys, had been joined in marriage—what would you expect?

Samuel Cony served in many positions including probate judge, state treasurer, and mayor of Augusta. In 1862, he was elected governor by a considerable majority. An ardent supporter of the Union, he sent more than 70,000 troops to fight in the war. He died in 1870.

The Samuel Cony House on Stone Street in Augusta dates from 1846 and is extant, occupying a huge tract, once an orchard, in the middle of the city. On Cony's death, it passed to Joseph Manley, who built a large barn, designed by John Calvin Stevens. The property was later acquired by the wealthy Viles family and is now preserved as part of the Viles Foundation, a philanthropic organization. The Vileses remodeled and enlarged the Italianate mansion in the Colonial style.

The four children of Joseph and Susan Manley spent summers at the family cottage at Small Point. Samuel Cony Manley was born in 1867, Lucy in 1869, Harriet in 1873, and Sydney Sewall in 1874. Lucy was named for her aunt, Lucy Cony, whose mother was Lucy Brooks, whom Samuel Cony married in 1849 following the death of Mercy Sewall. Joseph Bodwell's son, Joseph Fox Bodwell, had no issue.

Sydney Manley was an accomplished photographer, who kept a darkroom in the cellar of the cottage and took numerous photographs of family groups. We reproduce two examples in this history, a little perplexed by the fact that some of the numbers

Photograph of the Manley family group by Sydney Manley. *From left*: Samuel Manley, Harriet, Lucy, Chase Mellen, Susan C. Manley, and Joseph; *seated, far right*: Sydney.

Photograph of the holiday group at the Manley Cottage by Sydney Manley. *From left*: Joseph Manley holding Chase Mellen, and Lucy Manley Mellen; *seated*: Susan C. Manley, Col. Watson, Sydney Manley, plus friends and neighbors. (*courtesy of Jack Ijams*)

An early view of the Manley Cottage, *c*. 1889. (*Trott coll., LH*)

shown are clearly beyond those of the immediate family. Family descendants have been helpful, but I missed a generation who would have easily identified everyone.

JOHN OWEN PATTEN

The death of Joseph Bodwell temporarily halted the promotion and development of "Cliffstone." A notable exception was the impressive Queen Anne-style cottage built about 1893 for John Owen Patten of Bath.

The Patten family was already prominent and successful by 1861 when John Patten was born, having built ships at their yard on the banks of the Kennebec near North Street. John's interest in journalism took him to Boston where he was a reporter for the *Boston Post*. He invested in the paper and became managing editor. In 1886, he married Lucy Larrabee, daughter of a Bath attorney. They celebrated with a trip around the world.

In 1893, Patten and his wife returned to Bath, following the death of his wealthy grandfather. He acquired the *Bath Times* and was active in banking. In 1888, he founded the Sagadahoc Club, an exclusive men's social club, of which the likes of Gen. Thomas W. Hyde were members. He added to his newspaper holdings the *Sentinel* and the *Independent*, keeping the last name.

Socially prominent, Patten was the focus of local gossip when he and Lucy divorced (not common in the 1890s). John had been the patient of a New York physician named Percy Roberts, who moved with his wife, Irene, to Bath. John was diagnosed with tuberculosis.

Roberts and his wife also divorced, and not long thereafter, John Patten and the former Lucy Roberts were married. A custody case ensued over the five-year-old Roberts twins.

Following lengthy court proceedings, Irene won custody, save for the summer months, when the twins would live with their father at Small Point.

All of which caused a stir in Bath. Needless to say, neither the *Times* nor the weekly *Independent* gave coverage to the unfolding drama, but other publications not controlled by Patten made the most of it. John Patten's health was failing. In 1897, he sold his newspapers to Frank Nichols and moved to Boston. In 1899, he died of tuberculosis at the age of thirty-eight.

The Patten cottage at Small Point was named "Merrymeeting." An article in the *Independent* shows the cottage shortly after its completion, with family members posing beside it. References to Small Point are scarce; "The Last of His Generation" states that "During his [Patten's] residence at Bath his home at North and Front Streets and his summer home at Cape Small were two of the most hospitable homes of Bath."

An air of mystery surrounds the ownership of "Merrymeeting" after Patten's death. A deed shows that in 1901, a man named George O. Curtis of Brookline, Massachusetts, purchased the cottage and some abutting land, the latter from the estate of Governor Bodwell. He held the property for twenty-five years, then sold it to Harrison Wright in 1926. I had not seen the name until Bill Hoffman told me about the deed; he had not heard of Mr. Curtis. According to the 1900 Census, he lived in Boston with his mother and sister, was born in July 1875, and was single. His name does not appear in the register of the Small Point Club, which is unusual for a property owner. There is no reason to think that George Curtis was in any way related to Edward and Agnes Curtis, even though George's mother's name was Agnes.

Situated on a knoll south of the Manley Cottage, "Merrymeeting" had a splendid view of the beach and ocean which could be enjoyed from the long veranda. As proof, we offer a view of the cottage from the beach, a postcard dated 1908. By my time at Small Point, oak and black spruce trees had all but blocked that view, the fate likewise of the Manley and Bodwell Cottages.

In this later view, you can see that the veranda has been fully enclosed. The cottage itself was demolished in 1960, following the death of Mrs. Wright. Her daughter, Marie Hoffman, had a modern house constructed on the slope below the cottage site, which was subsequently remodeled and improved by her son, Billy, and his wife, Jan. Other family members had already built or acquired their own places, not that that excuses the destruction of an important historic house.

William Reed, a Boston entrepreneur with Maine connections, had a Queen Anne-style cottage built on the beach side of the newer road, below Bodwell's. This—along with "Merrymeeting," the Manson Cottage, the Anderson Cottage, and Spinney's Inn—completed the community around 1895, prior to the construction of the Small Point Club.

Thanks to Cathy Hoffman, I have an original copy of the 1896 map titled "Plan of Land at Cape Small Point Maine/Morton and Quimby, Civil Engineers and Landscape Architects/Boston, Jan. 1, 1896." Note that this plan was produced nine years after the death of Joseph Bodwell. It is not labeled "Cliffstone," or Bodwell and Spinney, but there are indications of the partition of the lands that settled the estate of Bodwell. The plan is a valuable document identifying the structures completed as of 1896.

The Bodwell Cottage is labeled B. F. Watson and has by far the largest lot. Others are J. H. Manley, J. O. Patten, S. Anderson, W. G. Reed, and Manson. Spinney's Inn is shown but not identified; the "P. O." is shown with the name Chase. The Harding lot

Photographs of "Merrymeeting," exterior shortly after completion, living room; collection of Elisabeth Trott (*courtesy of Libby Hills*)

Postcard view, "Merrymeeting" from the beach

is identified, with no structure. There are 153 numbered lots; the numbers probably include the improved ones listed above.

This poses an interesting legal question: was this plan registered, and if so, are the roads connecting the lots still rights of way and not to be blocked or built upon, regardless of their never being actually constructed as roads? I lived for a time in Cape Neddick, part of York, in a similar cottage development called "York Cliffs" (there were in fact no cliffs). Here, the unbuilt roads were treated as rights of way as shown on a plan. My house, "Sunset Hill," nearly encroached upon such a "paper road" right of way.

Seal Cove Road, which lacked an official name until around 1960, appears on the 1896 map, but its original date is uncertain, and it did not always extend as far as the Dearborn Camp (later the road was sometimes labeled "the Road to Dearborn's"). At the time the Gun Club was moved to Small Point, it could be reached only via the beach road, over the exposed sand in front of the High Rocks to the end of "Sewall's Beach", where a road connected to the end of the point. It was strictly low-tide access. Was Harold Sewall responsible for construction the connecting link, via "Ice Box Bend"? The curious name of this sharp bend in the road comes from a time—maybe 1938—when a hurricane swelled a brook and washed out the road and Mrs. Dearborn produced an abandoned wooden ice box to fill the gap.

A water supply was included in the "Cliffstone" development plan. From the Wyman ice pond, water was pumped to a tank on a tower and piped in 4-inch galvanized iron pipe to the various roads. The water was plentiful and, at least in later years, considered pure, but it was usually the color of tea. Some 5-gallon glass carboys of drinking water were available at Wyman's Store, together with metal swings to hold them and facilitate pouring out. Near the present-day tennis courts was a dug well with a hand pump. I remember going there with Dad and filling containers—probably not the 5-gallon variety.

Bodwell's ambitious plan remained for the most part a design on paper. Doubtless, the loss of his engaging and dynamic personality played a role in this decline, but similar developments that largely failed were common along the Maine Coast (and in Small Point).

Bodwell's cottage was of fairly simple design; it has a rectangular main block with a service ell to the rear, and, originally, open verandas on the two sides. Queen Anne-style detail was provided in turnings of the veranda posts and trim, diverse shingle patterns, and decorative brackets beneath the roof. Most of these features have been lost, but some remain on the carriage house, which is intact. They were also found on the general store, probably designed by the same person (not necessarily an architect). There are, fortunately, photographs of the Bodwell Cottage in its original state.

Some sources state that Bodwell ran a rooming house at his place. Elisabeth Trott's catalog of Small Point cottages contains a hand-written, unsigned document written in pencil on a portion of a program from the dedication of William Zorach's *The Spirit of the Sea*. The program is dated 1962, long after the era that it describes, yet the document is written with such a clear knowledge of its subject that we offer it here in its entirety. Yes, there is one glaring error: the cottage was built well after the Civil War and occupied by Bodwell's family until 1900.

The writer also provides genealogy for the Watson-McLanathan family, the colonel's first wife being Rebecca McLanathan, and his second wife being her niece, Mary. Here is the full text:

> The Watsons went first to the boarding house—sleeping in the house Watson later bought, dining in the Percy cottage, owned by Capt. Spinney who built the big room for a dining room. A board walk connected the 2 houses. About the time of the Civil War Watson bought the house, remodeling it into "Col. Watson's Japanese Mansion." This was before Arthur Sewall Sr. built the house across the road. Watson planted the spruces around the lot, built the stable, the stone entrance gates, laid out a croquet lawn next to the stable; guests arrived by boat from Boston, N.Y., etc, were met by a carriage driven by Sidney Eaton, with a wagon for the luggage driven by Wilbur Wyman (his first job!). Col. Watson flew the flags of the state, country, or etc. of the highest-ranking visitor. Guests left for an early boat Saturday; new guests arrived late the same Saturday! Every day servants moved the stuffed furniture, oriental rugs, etc. out onto the covered porches on three sides of the house. Col. W. built the widow's walk, cut off the corner for the window of the master bedroom, added the gargoyles.[1]

The covered verandas along the sides of the house were added by Watson. The front veranda was removed by the McLanathans, no doubt because "it made the living room so dark."

Bodwell's partner, Melville Spinney, took over the Abner Lowell House and turned it into Spinney's Inn. A large dining room addition to the rear, with a stone chimney and fireplace, provided space for the serving of shore dinners to guests and local summer

Postcard view of Wyman's Store and the Small Point Beach Post Office.

Photograph of "Sea Winnocks." (*courtesy of Elena Vandervoort*)

folk. The inn was going strong in 1900 when the Wright family visited Small Point. In a Christmas message *c.* 1986, Sibyl Wright Coates recalls:

> My first recollections of Small Point in or around 1900 was of Captain and Mrs. Spinney's boarding house (now the Percy House). I dimly remember the huge dining room with long tables where Mrs. Spinney served us our meals. Marie, myself and our parents—vanilla ice cream made a special hit with us children. In front of the house stands an enormous linden tree which in those early days had a swing attached to its branches. Capt. Spinney, with a red nose and jovial manner, used to swing us there!
>
> Father and Mother had come to Small Point at the suggestion of the Manleys—Mrs. Mellen and Mrs. Breck, daughters of Joseph H Manley of Augusta ...
>
> The older house next to the Manleys (now the Vandervoorts) was owned by a Colonel Watson. In the top was a so-called "Widow's Watch," now done away with. Colonel Watson had constructed a narrow boardwalk leading from the back of his house through the meadow to the road between Wyman's store and the Spinneys (for meals). The boardwalk has long ago vanished. Wyman's store, however, endured through many generations of Wymans ...
>
> Up the hill from the Spinney-Percy house stood the Wyman house, across from which was their huge barn. It was from their cows that, for years, we had our milk—non-pasteurized and delivered daily in huge milk cans. The Wymans also had an ice house in a field nearby supplying Small Point with ice for our non-electric ice chests.[2]

The value of a document like this one is beyond measure. Sybil's memories of Spinney's Inn go back to when she was probably four years old. A news item, presumably from the *Bath Independent*, reveals another side of Melville Spinney, dated April 1894:

> Dr. Anderson, one day last week, was at Small Point visiting his cottage, when, taking a strol [*sic.*] down to see the surf break on the beach, much to his astonishment he saw in a little cockle shell of a boat that, half the time, seemed to be standing on end, the plump and manly figure of Landlord Spinney. Mr. Spinney was grasping the gunwale of the boat with one hand and shooting coot with the other.
>
> It looked like a dangerous business, but Mr. Spinney was firing onto the birds as if enjoying life.
>
> When Landlord Spinney came ashore, he unloaded 26 coot from the boat with the remark "that it was roughest weather for coot shooting that he ever saw."

The year 1894 saw the SS *City of Lowell* delivered to a New York operator. This was the first steel-hulled commercial vessel built by Bath Iron Works. The same newspaper notes that workers are "rushing along their work" on the ship, putting in eleven hours a day.

My Cape Neddick house was part of "York Cliffs" development (there were no cliffs), which consisted of large summer cottages built for members of the corporation or for rental. A substantial summer hotel, the Passaconnaway Inn was constructed, so the rental houses did not need kitchens. The development identified dozens of cottage lots, but few were ever sold. The Inn lasted a mere forty-two years before being demolished for salvage. My house, called "Sunset Hill," was built in 1897 for John D. Vermeule. A splendid Queen Anne-style mansion, it had fallen into disrepair and gave me my first major restoration job.

It is interesting to compare Joseph Bodwell and Melville Spinney's development of Small Point with what happened somewhat later at nearby Sebasco to the northwest. In 1909, a wealthy New York businessman named Freeman H. Merritt purchased Horse Island, directly across the harbor from the present-day resort. He laid out a system of roads and cottage lots, and eventually also acquired a substantial additional acreage on the mainland.

Merritt immediately began constructing cottages (called "bungalows"), a large one for his use being, interestingly, on the mainland. The cottages were available for rent, not for sale, and were promptly occupied by New Yorkers and others.

The cottages were finished on the exterior with slabs that retained their bark, or more specifically, logs that were custom sawn for the purpose in Merritt's own sawmill on site. The attached bark was treated with "a solution of soft soap and carbolic acid to keep out the bugs." The effect was more like a log cabin than a traditional bungalow, though they did have the typical large, covered front porch that was a feature of the bungalow style. Each cottage had a massive chimney made of local beach stones with a fireplace 5 feet wide. Quite possibly, George Dearborn visited "Ocean Highlands," as the development was called (by Mr. Merritt at least) and decided to use the same slabs with bark on at his camp at Small Point.

In addition to the cottage community of Sebasco Estates, Freeman Merritt had extensive farming operations as well as a successful hotel that became Sebasco Lodge. He was clearly willing and able to make a huge investment in the whole project, and it paid off. No question, he started out with a far better site than "York Cliffs." Bodwell did not build cottages for rental, though there came to be a demand for rentals at Small Point. His untimely death in 1887 put everything on hold, including plans for a grand hotel.

THE SMALL POINT CLUB

On 30 August 1895, Joseph Manley wrote the Articles of Association, "To own and maintain a club-house at Phippsburg ... for our mutual social intercourse" and gave the following names: Joseph H. Manley, Harry H. Stinson, Joseph F. Bodwell, and Malcolm S. Holway.

He called a meeting for September 16 at his Phippsburg residence. On August 24, the initial shareholders met at Small Point, purchasing one or two shares at $300 apiece. In addition to those named were Samuel Cony Manley, son of Joseph; Orville D. Baker, former attorney general of Maine; Wm. G. Reed; Arthur Sewall; and John A. Patten (probably John O.).

My painting shows the club as it appeared immediately after construction, in 1897. Later, a wing was added at the left rear.

The senior members of this corporation were all deeply involved in state politics, though not all held elected office. Founder Joseph Manley was, in the words of his granddaughter Sydney Breck Smith, "a politician behind the scenes." In those days, candidates for office were selected by committees of prominent men such as these.

Opening Day. (Painting, TH)

Mr. Manley served as postmaster of Augusta, in which position he was able to collect commissions on the handling of large mailings. His weekly journal, *The Maine Farmer*, was widely read. He lived in style on the vast farm right in the midst of the city.

It would be appropriate to call the Small Point Club as conceived a Republican men's club. No doubt, Mrs. Manley, having been surrounded by politics all her life, was pleased to have political gatherings moved out of the house.

Joseph Fox Bodwell and Samuel Cony Manley were sons of Joseph Manley and the late Joseph Bodwell, and they seemed less interested in politics. The young Bodwell was elected president of the club corporation and served in that capacity until his death in 1915.

At the meeting on September 16, it was voted to purchase the land and "build a club-house thereon." On May 29, 1897, the shareholders voted to "accept the Club-House as built and furnished by the Executive Committee." The capitalization by sale of shares was $9,000, and the corporation approved issuing "notes of the corporation" in the amount of $2,500. Thus the cost of the land and building, furnished, was $11,500, or about $700,000 in today's dollars.

As late as 1927, the minutes of meetings of the Corporation were written in longhand. In 1927, the members voted to construct a garage near Wyman's store, the cost not to exceed $1,000, and to look into the possibility of having electric lighting. The architect for the club was Joseph L. Neal of Pittsburgh, who had designed the impressive Lithgow Library in Augusta and so was known to the corporation members. His original design for the exterior, which might be called "stick Style with Tudor influence," was not executed, probably in an effort to simplify and reduce cost. The *Industrial Journal* published the following description on October 9, 1896:

> One of the additions to Maine's summer homes for this season ... is the new club house at Small Point, owned by 12 Augusta gentlemen, who organized the Small Point Club in 1895 and had the house built this year by Capt. Charles H. McIntyre of Small Point. The building is three stories high, furnished outside with a splendid overhanging roof of 3 ft., overhung with ornamental brackets and diamond points. Lower story clapboarded. The second story commences with a 10 inch band and 4 1/2 inch crown molding and crazy shingles up to tip with a plain band of 9 inches between second and third stories. Having 6 double A windows, three on each side, with a fine piazza 10 ½ feet, 30 feet upon each side, extending across the east side. This building is finished on the inside, the lower front consisting of a dining room 20 × 40, library 20 × 20, kitchen 20 × 20, with a pantry and hall finished in yellow pine. The second has 24 rooms including two cozy bath rooms with set tubs furnished in single and double suites with white wood. On the third floor are 23 fine rooms, including two more bath rooms finished all with whitewood and wainscoting of yellow pine finished in natural color, presenting a neat and tidy appearance. The bath rooms are painted above the wainscoted walls and ceiling a pale blue, greatly adding to the fine appearance of these rooms.

Regrettably, nearly all of the "fish scale" and alternating or "crazy" shingles have been replaced by plain courses.

The club was in fact equipped with fifteen guest rooms on two floors. Bathrooms, two per floor, were located at the rear end of the central corridor; thus, the best rooms, at the front, had the longest walk to the bathroom. Today, there are still no private bathrooms, and guests soon get used to the walk.

Originally intended to be a small men's club, the Small Point Club became the gathering place for a growing community, and expansion and alterations were in order. In July 1904, the board voted to borrow $6,000 to construct and furnish an addition—namely, the ell containing the dining room and expanded service rooms, with staff quarters on the second floor. The existing building allowed for no access for guests to a new wing to the south, due to the placement of the kitchen at the "rear."

So the dining room was reached by an open veranda leading from "the Cage." This exotically named space is the glass-enclosed southeast corner of the veranda, and it has always been the cocktail lounge. Originally, it was the location of an oak cabinet with compartments in which members kept their spirits. The founders had their initials painted on their cabinet door. More details will follow in a later chapter.

Exterior detail matched the existing building, second-floor dormers having the bracketed A-style. Yet the interior was more camp-like, lacking plaster or wainscot, the framing and sheathing simply stained dark green. The exposed framing and somewhat rough sheathing gave the room a rustic flavor out of keeping with the original, finished rooms. The framing was minimal, and the floor still has a bounce. The fashion for white paint in the 1960s just made it all worse.

In 1910, a telephone was installed, one of two at Small Point. An outside door was added to provide direct access; the door remains unused. In 1912, Harold Sewall was appointed to look into moving the stairs, which descended into the center of the lobby. The change was carried out by a local contractor named Joseph Wyman, brother of Martin Wyman of Small Point. The stairs were relocated behind the chimney and the lobby turned into a spacious living room, the scene of countless parties.

In 1924, the membership voted to cover the "piazza" leading to the dining room. Much later, when I was a director, it was fully enclosed for use as extended dining space. There was also talk of improving the large open space "under the southeast corner of the piazza," but this did not happen.

With but a few later alterations, and some unfortunate attempts at modern paint colors for the interior, the club carries on. The community could use a large meeting hall. We return to Sibyl Coates's essay for a remarkable early recollection:

> From about 1902 the Wright family spent summers at the Small Point Club, ... built circa 1889–1900 by a group of men from Augusta—friends of the Manleys.... I believe that the men were all bachelors! Just to mention a few names—Orville Baker, Mel Holway, Jim Marvine, etc. Our names were soon entered in the Club register, joining a Mrs. Goodwin from Augusta, and various "Coneys" [*sic.*] related to the Manleys. We had rooms on the third floor for years. Room furniture consisted of two beds, one bureau and a wash-stand decorated on top with basin, pitcher, soap dish and mug. In the lower portion, doors opened to display a "slop jar," and the inevitable "potty," necessary sometimes because, on each floor, there were only two bathrooms at the far end of the hall. No electricity or telephone in those days! Affixed to the bureau was a small kerosene lamp on a brass fixture.[3]

It is curious that she misspells "Cony," the name of the prominent Augusta family whom the Baldwins probably knew. Jim Marvine is a mystery.

Sibyl is not quite accurate; not all of the founders were bachelors, certainly not Joseph Manley. Yet there were several single men, including the Manley and Bodwell sons, and educated career government officials like Melvin Holway, a Bowdoin and Harvard graduate trained in the law. A modern-day reader might ask if these men were in fact gay; I have no reason to think so and would say that they enjoyed getting together for cards and drinks and to talk over the business of the state. A clubhouse was the ideal venue.

ANOTHER DEVELOPER ON THE SCENE

Joseph Bodwell was not the only developer to take a fancy to Small point. In 1893, the Mountain Farm and Sea-Shore Company was started by four Bath investors with a view to creating an immense summer community on Morse's Mountain and along Seawall Beach. They produced a site map showing 600 lots, a system of roads, and even a trolley line (no indication of where it originated). A fancy brochure described the features of the land in sumptuous prose, Seawall Beach being "unequalled for surf-bathing by any other of the New England Coast ... and where two thousand people can disport themselves amidst the billows without jostling." Had their development been realized, Small Point would have become another York Beach.

The enterprise failed. The developers negotiated the purchase of the lands of the various Morse holders and the Sprague property to the west. The sellers were never paid in full, if at all. The network of roads was barely begun; a road of sorts led to the summit, which had served as a military lookout, but there was no way for prospective buyers to view most of the lots. Buyers did not appear, despite the glowing brochure. Clearly, the four men lacked sufficient capitalization, hoping that advance sales would make the difference.

The trolley track on the developers' plan seems ridiculous and yet the possibility of a rail line of some sort between Bath and Small Point was taken seriously, leading to the creation in 1891 of the Bath, Small Point and Popham Beach Railroad, Inc.—a company made up of businessmen from Portland, Augusta, and Waterville. They claimed to have funding in place, and given that this line could be public transportation, they would have been in a position to take land for the right-of-way by eminent domain. The plan never evolved, but in 1896, yet another group from Bath revived the idea and brought in engineers and experts to study the terrain. A narrow-gauge railway was their recommendation; such a rail system was already in place, not far away: the Waterville, Wiscasset, and Farmington Railway. The narrow gauge allowed for a steam-powered line with smaller locomotives and rolling stock—a considerable saving. No doubt, the Mountain and Sea-Shore people were involved.

An electric trolley would have copied a system well established in Maine, linking most cities and towns. In this case, the lack of a ready source of electric power at the southern end may have ruled it out. More importantly, there was no existing demand for a transportation system that would have been enormously expensive to construct, only the potential for such a demand. The potential demand for cottage lots had not panned out. So, the Morses stayed on, quietly farming their mountain, and so, after a fashion, did the Spragues.

Jethro Sprague was the first of his family to settle in Small Point, where he had the good fortune to marry the daughter of Nathaniel Sylvester. He purchased a large piece of farmland lying between the Sprague River marsh and the harbor, bordering on the south by land of Isaiah Wyman, on the north by that of Sylvester. Jethro probably had a small hall and parlor house on the rise to the north, of which the frame may survive as an ell to a larger dwelling dating from the 1830s. To that unit was added by James Sprague a typical 1870s two-and-a-half-story Victorian house. Thus there are three periods joined in an example of "connected architecture." However, the barn was located across the present road.

There were at least two branches of the family: Nelson Sprague had a cape and barn on the shore of the Back Bay, now the path of the highway but with old apple trees bearing witness. The house, dating from the 1790s, is seen in a photograph by Emma Sewall, *c.* 1900, but it was lost not long after. In the 1950s, the state highway was relocated across the site of the Nelson Sprague house. It previously ran close to the marsh, curving sharply to the left (southbound) at the Back Bay and then to the right, connecting with the beach road, then passing up the hill to the store and the Club Road.

Catalog illustration, "Mountain & Shore Development."

The Sprague homestead, painting by Patt Trott. (*Coll. TH*)

This raises the question—did the road ever pass in front of the Sylvester House? It is unusual for such an early house to be built on a dead-end lane. Did the road then run to the east of the Sprague field, thus eliminating those sharp curves? Such a route would have avoided having the main road cut through the Sprague farm. I have found no early map to answer this question. History is never done.

"Improvements" to roads were common; the road to Popham originally ran along what is now Bodwell Grange Road, then curved to the left behind the Daniel Blaisdell House and became the current route. A new beginning of the Popham Road was more direct, and the old road was abandoned in 1944.

Until the 1950s, the pavement ended at Sprague Road and the highway south was a narrow, dusty road. By "pavement," we do not mean the smoothly rolled asphalt of today. Early rural coating was called "tar and gravel," though the gravel was more like sand. A thick, oily tar was sprayed on the road, then mixed with sand by a grader, and finally a coating of sand was applied to the surface, intended to reduce the spray of tar onto one's car.

The Dearborn Road, now Seal Cove Road, was so narrow that two vehicles could not pass, one having to turn into a driveway. Poorly drained, the surface was subject to huge puddles when it rained.

Jethro's nephew, James Sprague had two children, James, Jr., and Vilora. Following a common pattern in Small Point families, she married Loring Gilman, whose family still live in the northern part of Small Point where the church is located. Three generations later came Stanwood Gilman, co-author with his wife, Margaret, of the Small Point history and a direct descendant of Jethro Sprague.

It was, of course, assumed that James, Jr., would continue to operate the farm, following a career as a seaman, as Abner Lowell had done. Unfortunately, he was lost at sea. That left Vilora, who had no desire to live on the farm and was happy to sell to the Mountain and Seashore people. When that enterprise collapsed, Bradford Sprague (a cousin from Bath who had invested some money in that venture), realizing that there was no money left, settled instead for the family farm property and moved to Small Point with his daughter, Bessie.

After the death of her father, Bessie maintained the farm, keeping horses and cows in the new barn that James had built near the house. In 1927, the Spragues, aware of changes taking place in Small Point, sold a parcel on the branch to John and Kate Chandler from Sterling, Massachusetts, who built a large camp. Yet the conveyance stated that Sprague cattle were to be allowed to graze on all but a fenced yard in front of the house. One might have a cow at the bedroom window.

Finally, in 1957, the balance of the Sprague property was sold by Bessie to a consortium of summer residents, including Chase Mellen, Jr., William Sanford, Nathan Lord, and Baldwin Terry. Chase Mellen, known as "Junie," envisioned the large tract

Aerial photograph of the Sprague farm, *c.* 1930. (*courtesy of B. White*)

along the harbor as a place for the summer community to expand. It did so but slowly; there was still considerable untouched land along the east side. An article in *The Bath Independent* of May 27, 1899, chronicles the earlier growth of the summer community:

> The cottages are situated in a general northerly direction from this building [the Club], the newest of them being that of Hon. Arthur Sewall of Bath having been built last year and to be occupied for the first time at the beginning of the present season. The others are owned by Hon. Joseph H. Manley of Augusta, the Pattens of Bath, Colonel B. F. Watson of New York, William Gardner Reed, Esq. of Boston, Dr. Samuel Anderson of Bath, and Mrs. George F. Manson of Boston. It is probable that at least one more cottage will be built during 1899. There is also a boarding house kept by Captain Melville B. Spinney and a family supply store conducted by William D. Coombs, steward of the Club, and a Post Office which is served by two daily mails....

11

The Sewall Family

This brings us to the Sewall family. In her excellent survey of early houses, *Historic Homes of New England*, Mary Northend writes:

> One of the first settlers at Newbury, Massachusetts, was one Henry Sewall, who came over from England in 1634, bringing with him cattle, servants, and provisions. He was allotted six hundred acres of upland and marsh land at Newbury, according to agreement made before he left his native country.

The grant was later divided into several lots, one of which was acquired by William Longfellow, who married Anne Sewall. This family connection was to be followed in the early twentieth century.

A branch of the Sewall family moved to York Village in Maine around 1720. The Nicholas Sewall House occupies a prominent position in the center of town. I purchased it in 1984 and did considerable restoration of the interior, which was largely intact but battered—a crossing of paths.

ARTHUR SEWALL

Arthur Sewall's name appears on the 1896 list of founders of the Small Point Club. He and his brother, Edward, were patriarchs of a large and important Bath family. The brothers worked together for a few years, but their personalities were incompatible; Edward was relaxed and imaginative, while Arthur was a businessman of focus and determination. His company built and owned sailing ships, which is to say that he personally supervised not only their construction but the hiring of captains and planning of voyages. Curiously, he was a Democrat among Republicans, and, still more curiously, the party chose him to run for vice president with the eccentric William Jennings Bryan. In those days, candidates were chosen behind closed doors, not by public polls as they are, more or less, today. Sewall seemed (at least to the Democratic Party) a steady New Englander, just what was needed for balance. The Bryan-Sewall ticket was defeated.

As Bath's first family, the Sewall men considered public service a privilege and a responsibility, if at a more local level than the vice presidency. For the next two generations, they nearly all appear in state and local positions.

Unfortunately, Mr. Sewall totally lacked political skills; his personality was scarcely outgoing or genial. He was heartily disliked by his blue-collar workers. In any case, the 1896 election was won by William McKinley, and Arthur Sewall returned to his ships, taking an increased interest in Small Point. He purchased the portion of the Sprague farm bordering the Sprague Marsh and the existing Greenleaf cottage, which predated the Bodwell era.

It was not until 1898 that Sewall and his wife, Emma Crooker Sewall, commissioned a splendid cottage overlooking the Sprague Marsh called "The Dunes," designed by Boston architects Kendall, Taylor and Stevens in the "Colonial style," now known as "Colonial Revival." By this time, their two sons, Harold and William, were also deeply involved in Small Point acquisitions. Without question, this family secured the preservation of Small Point and put an end to any threat that Bodwell's elaborate development plan might be realized.

William "Will" Sewall came to own at least 50 acres between the beach road and the marsh, and his brother, Harold, had the land at the southern end of what is now Seal Cove Road and west to land of the Wyman family. These two large tracts provided sites for cottages for Sewall family members for decades to come. In addition, Arthur's sister Alice owned a beach-front lot below the club where she built a cottage around 1895.

Photograph of Arthur Sewall at "The Dunes," by E. Sewall. (*AS*)

Harold also owned the Wildes Farm about 1 mile north on the main road—another large property with distant ocean views (at least in his day).

Arthur Sewall died in 1901, and Emma continued to occupy "The Dunes." Emma Sewall was a highly regarded photographer whose subjects included scenes that included Small Point farmers and fishermen. Given the limitations of film in 1900, her subjects had to hold still while being photographed. She won awards for her work, and her great-granddaughter, Abbie Sewall, published a volume of her photographs entitled *Message Through Time*. "The Dunes" remains in the family, owned by Polly Hyde Crawford, a direct descendant.

The Alice Sewall Cottage was acquired by William Sewall, who gave it to his daughter, Dorothy, as a wedding present. The cottage was totally destroyed by fire on March 27, 1953. Dorothy Jayne had it rebuilt, and it has been expanded by her daughter, Pam Miller, and Pam's husband, Don.

The loss of the Alice Sewall Cottage had profound consequences for my family. The lot that Harrison Wright had sold to my parents was in the woods, on a rise of some 40 feet, directly above the Jaynes. One day, when "Dolly" Jayne was at our house, she remarked, "I think you could have a view"—of the water, that is. She said that we could top a few spruce trees growing on her side of the Club Road.

In those days, *c.* 1950, we had a crew of men from Bath Iron Works who came down on Saturdays to do tree work and general maintenance. When one offered to fix an electrical problem, my mother asked, "Are you an electrician?" to which he replied, "I wire destroyers." In other words, they were men of many skills.

In this case, the men became arborists and climbed the trees and cut off the tops and we had suddenly a glimpse of shining blue water, only a glimpse. Then Dolly's house burned, and with it many trees, greatly expanding our view, and in the fall of that year came not one but two hurricanes—Carol and Edna. Now, our view was panoramic. The trees began to grow back of course, but the Millers had a second cottage built along with a parking area, and once again, we had a truly awesome view, with Seguin Island exactly in the center. Our site being elevated some 40 feet above the Club Road, we looked over the Miller houses below and were not aware of their presence.

Another recollection of life at the club comes from Dick Kelley, who is the author of a memoir of growing up in the Wynberg community of Phippsburg, near the Basin. Hurricane Carol struck on August 31, 1954:

> It was the end of my second season as "houseboy." I was ready to head off to my freshman year in college ... And then the hurricane hit.
>
> The driving rain and hurricane force winds started in the afternoon, into the evening and went on for at least a full day. If you walked into the lobby of the club you found the rug hovering and flapping about a foot off the floor as the wind under the club pushed up through the floorboards. The rain water came right through the clapboards of the building and through the plaster walls. You could barely stand up if you walked outside.
>
> Small Point was a mess. Trees down. Power out. Wind damage to cottages. The galvanized water pipes which carried fresh water to the cottages were broken.... At the Club, the cocktail lounge ["The Cage"] was virtually gone. Water stains throughout the walls. To flush toilets for ourselves and the few remaining guests we carried buckets of

> sea water up the stairs and dumped them into the toilet tanks. Not a lot of fun. The most bizarre thing to me was the strange mixture of salt, sand, and shredded leaves which covered almost everything as much as an eighth of an inch thick. Windows which faced east and had not broken or blown out were covered with this strange stuff.[1]

I must take exception to one sentence of Dick's colorful narrative: the wind may have lifted the carpets when the door was open, but the air did not come "through the floorboards." The club has good, solid hard pine flooring. Dick mentions Barbara Wyman as being one of the club staff as she was earlier during Aunt Polly's tenure. Barbara was the daughter of Swanton and Peggy Wyman, and she grew up in what is now our house. She was later a teacher in Massachusetts. Edith Young was manager when the hurricane struck. Our friend, Dick Kelly, died early in 2019. He was an ardent supporter of historic preservation and served for many years as chairman of the town commission.

HAROLD M. SEWALL

Harold Marsh Sewall was a U.S. representative to the republic of Hawaii, long before the islands became a state. He was involved in shipping between the islands and the west coast. After his father's death, he returned to Bath, where he had built a splendid house and indulged his passion for Small Point where he had built "Camp Sabino," originally the work of the Boston architect, William Longfellow (a cousin). It was a large but basic camp, as well as the scene of big parties. Legend has it that after the festivities ended, a curtain would be drawn across the main room, with men sleeping on one side, women on the other.

Harold M. Sewall. (*courtesy of Sewall Janeway*)

Harold Sewall, being of a maritime family, became a collector of antiques and paintings related to the sea, and "Camp Sabino" soon resembled a museum. The artifacts included carved wooden figureheads from the large, square-rigged sailing ships, among which was a larger than life Scotsman with bagpipes, which was placed every summer at the end of the driveway (clearly, security was not a major concern). It scared the hell out of me as a small child.

The collection ultimately became the foundation of the Bath Marine Museum, originally housed in Harold Sewall's house on Washington Street, which later became the Maine Maritime Museum. The Scotsman, a unique and priceless antique, and his companions were safely bestowed here.

The family home, a Victorian mansion in the Italianate style, dating from 1874, was located at 1180 Washington Street. The architect was Francis Fassett, a Bath native who became Portland's leading architect of the 1870s and 1880s. No family member wanted to occupy it after Emma's death in 1919, and it stood vacant until 1935 when it was demolished. Later, the modern Grace Episcopal Church was constructed on the site.

Harold's house, in the Colonial style, remained in the family until his daughter, Camilla Edge, gave it to the museum. After the museum moved to its new campus on the Kennebec, the house passed to Camilla Sewall Wood, who operated an events center there. For several years, the place was vacant and in deteriorating condition; in 2015, it was placed upon the "Most Endangered List of Maine Preservation." Then, a new owner saved it.

Harold Sewall had two sons—Arthur Sewall II and Loyall Farragut Sewall—and two daughters—Kaiulani and Camilla. His wife was Camilla Ashe of California. The Hawaiian name comes from the Hawaiian princess whom Harold came to know, and the three names appear repeatedly among daughters of the family. Kaiulani married John Williams and had a cottage across the road from "Camp Sabino," which remains in her family. Loyall took over the camp and enlarged it. Camilla married Senator Edge of New Jersey and received the Wildes Farm as a wedding present. She and Walter Edge transformed a typical 1830s farm into a magnificent country estate with a saltwater swimming pool. Arthur never built a cottage at Small Point.

Harold Sewall was an ardent conservationist. At the time of his death in 1924, he owned all of the interior land to the west of Seal Cove Road, extending to the ocean at Shell Beach and bordered on the west by lands of the Wyman family. His brother's estate held the strip of land at the end of the road beginning at the state highway, previously owned by Melville Spinney. The choice beachfront acres were owned by family members and by the Dearborns. The remaining large tract was probably intended by Harold to remain in complete conservation; his will established what was called "Harold Sewall Undivided." No doubt, this became a financial burden to the heirs, and in the 1970s, the land was divided, with heirs of Arthur II receiving an extensive parcel along the Navy Road. They made up for lack of presence in the community; Harold's daughter Ceci Janeway built a large camp near "Ice Box Bend," which was inherited by her son, Sewall Janeway, and his sister, Ashley. Later, Sewall had his own cottage built next door. Other relatives built down the Navy Road. Would Harold have approved? He would not have approved of the Navy Road. We shall return to the Navy Road under "military history."

A remarkable change did take place when the Lee and MacFadyen families, heirs of Camilla Edge, agreed to place the entire southern tip of Small Point under a permanent conservation easement and thereby ruling out possible development of as many as thirty lots on the 40 acres. The community has grown to the point where conservation is truly urgent; there just is not "room for everyone to build."

WILLIAM D. SEWALL

William D. "Will" Sewall built the impressive "York Hall" on Edward Street, just off Washington, in Bath, in 1897. Standing on Sewall Hill, it overlooks the William D. Sewall House of his grandfather, which also remained in the family. When I saw the interior of York Hall in about 2005, it was remarkably intact. It has since had a succession of owners.

William D. Sewall occupied "The Dunes" following the death of his mother and controlled some 50 acres bordering Sprague River and marsh.

Harold and Will Sewall continued to operate the family's ship-building yard after Arthur's death, well into the twentieth century. Their ships remained schooners, powered by the wind, though with steel hulls. They believed, like their father, that the requirements of steam power, the engine and the space taken by storage of coal for it, simply took too much cargo space. Finally, in 1912, they closed the yard and leased it

"The Dunes." (*TH*)

to the Texas Company. Oil was clearly the trend. Texaco built tankers for several years in the yard. William D. Sewall died in a motor vehicle accident in 1933.

Will Sewall also named his first son Arthur—how to distinguish him from Arthur Sewall II? Will's son was known as "Too-ie," which neither I nor anyone knew exactly how to spell; a "W" would simply have made matters worse. A second son was Sumner, whose military and political careers will warrant a chapter. Daughter Dorothy ("Dolly"), a very small woman, received her aunt Alice's cottage as a wedding present when she married John Kennon Jayne.

SUMNER SEWALL

Sumner Sewall was a man of big ideas and boundless energy. With the outbreak of World War I, he volunteered in the French Ambulance Service, but his military career took off when he joined the 95th Aero Squadron of the U.S. Army. This was the first military use of aircraft, and Sewall made brilliant use of it, shooting down a number of German planes and becoming an "Ace" pilot. He was awarded the *Croix de Guerre,* the *Legion d'Honneur*, and other medals by the grateful French.

Another member of the 95th Aero Squadron was Quentin Roosevelt, the youngest son of Theodore Roosevelt. His father relished the more dramatic elements of war and urged his four sons to enlist, which they did. Two were wounded, yet two fought again in World War II, where Theodore, Jr., led the troops at Utah Beach and died. Quentin, possessed of a wild streak, was a fearless and successful pilot like Sumner Sewall. On July 14, 1918, he was shot down and killed. Theodore died six months later, his love of combat lost to grief.

It is important to note that Sumner Sewall was not one of the so-called "Lafayette Esquadrille," a band of young Americans who knew how to fly and were given French planes—a clear violation of American law forbidding service in foreign armies but for which they were not prosecuted (my cousin, Frank Hinkle, was one of them). Immediately after the war ended, Sumner went to Berlin on a special assignment with the War Department (now the Department of Defense), taking his family with him.

Sumner Sewall became deeply involved in state politics, serving both as a state senator and a representative. In 1940, he was elected governor, serving two terms and thus missing any action in World War II. He was also president of Bath National Bank. In 1950, he purchased the entire Hermit Island at Small Point from the original Morse family owners (it had also been called Morse's Neck). Who was the hermit of Hermit Island? In Gloria Gray's *Small Point, Volume II*, an essay by historian Christopher Sewall, Sumner's grandson, identifies him as Albert Morse, the last resident of the island, formerly known as "Morse's Neck." He was a farmer and a genuine hermit, refusing to have dealings with anyone.

Gloria Gray includes newspaper accounts of a major fire on the island in August 1937. A second fire happened ten years later, in the year of devastating fires: 1947. My father manned a tent set up to watch for new outbreaks of fire, and, I am sure, he enjoyed a night of drink and conversation.

Hermit Island is a large tract of over 200 acres, connected to the mainland by a right of way over Head Beach that, at least years ago, was sometimes underwater at flood tide. There were a few cottages at the south end near the beach, and otherwise only one old house, long abandoned, near the north end. Brooke Lee organized "haunted house" events for us children using the derelict house as a setting. It was later demolished. The whole island was made into a campground, with various fishing enterprises along the inner shore. The notorious fire in 1947 had destroyed most of the island's forests, which made for fine views from every campsite. The campground has remained an immensely popular destination to this day.

Sumner Sewall married Helen Ellena who was born in Kovno, Russia, and left in 1918, living briefly in England with her British husband before leaving him and coming to the United States. According to one newspaper account, she was formerly Countess Makaravitch. According to another, she was born in Poland.

Ellena Sewall was a brilliant, theatrical personality who never lost her European accent and had memorable pronouncements on all matters. She took great interest in the marriage of her granddaughter, Elena Charles, to my friend, Bob Small, for which I was best man. "Oh, Tominkle," she exclaimed, "you come in green truck, I think you telephone man!" The Sewalls had three children—David, Nicholas, and Alaxandra, the last two names reflecting their mother's heritage.

Sumner Sewall ran for Senate in 1948 and was defeated by none other than Margaret Chase Smith. He left politics and continued to be active in the airline industry. Sumner died in 1965, aged only sixty-seven. City offices and a number of businesses closed during the funeral.

Here is another curious crossing of paths: the Sewall family originally settled in York. Nicholas Sewall was a tanner whose large house stands at the south end of the triangular cemetery in the town center. It dates from 1725. Needless to say, I was drawn to it, and in 1987, I was able to purchase it. It had many original features including a huge central chimney, but it was in dreadful shape.

I met my plumber, Harold Stevens, there and he said, "Tom, this place is a god-damned disaster!" I said, "Never mind, Harold, we will do the plumbing and heating from scratch." The Nicholas Sewall House remains, largely intact, surrounded by museum buildings, in York Village. Sumner's son, Nicky Sewall, was not named for his ancestor.

Sumner Sewall and his military career led to the presence of another Small Point family, that of General Edward P. Curtis, who in World War I was Sumner's fellow officer in the Air Corps, and like Sumner, an ace pilot. The following is from *Life with My Wife*, a tedious memoir by Horton O'Neil:

> On the 5th [July 1978] we had cocktails with Ted and Agnes Curtis and learned how Ted and Sumner Sewall had become friends as aviators in the Lafayette Quadrille [*sic.*], and how in 1937 when Sumner called him to say that the house next door could be had for seven thousand, Ted offered six and it was his the next day.

The house next door was the William Gardner Reed Cottage. Born in Waldoboro in 1858, Reed graduated from Bowdoin and studied law in Boston, where he became a respected attorney. In 1894, he commissioned Charles McIntyre to build a large cottage in the Queen Anne style. He had little use of the place, for not long after it was finished, he had become involved in a silver mine in Leadville, Colorado—a move that led him into bankruptcy. Joseph Manley got wind of these developments and told

Above: Newspaper photograph of Sumner Sewall with Ellena and Eleanor Roosevelt. (*LH*)

Left: Newspaper photograph of the Sumner Sewall family: Ellena, Nicholas, David, and Alexandra. (*Trott coll. LH*)

McIntyre to collect payment for the cottage as soon as possible. McIntyre did so. Mr. Reed "disappeared," according to a newspaper account; in fact, he changed his name and stayed out west.

The cottage was acquired by Oscar Sewall, son of Arthur's brother, Edward, then passed to his son Frank about 1933, then to Horace and Corinne Ropes, who were distant relatives of the Sewalls. They named the place "Ropes' End." The name has led some to assume that it was once the home of the landscape painter Joseph Ropes, but he was deceased by the time his grandson, Horace, got the property. The Small Point Club was able to purchase a painting of the beach below the club by Ropes, which Arthur Williams, himself an artist (and a Sewall cousin), spotted in a New York gallery.

"Ropes' End" remained for three generations in the Curtis family and was sold to Miguel Martin of the Manley family. The price was somewhat higher than $6,000. The house is intact, with additions. Mr. and Mrs. Curtis rebuilt the existing carriage house for their own use, and the family took over the main house. Grandson Curtis Henderson continues to live year-round in the carriage house.

The first person the Sewalls ever sold any of their land to an outsider to was George Dearborn.

THE DEARBORNS

George Dearborn was a friend of Harold Sewall from Hawaiian days. He worked in New York as a shipping agent, and in about 1900, he became the president of the American-Hawaiian Steamship Navigation Company, operating steamships and controlling the Hawaiian sugar trade. Harold's cousin, Oscar Sewall, son of Edward, was a director, as was Lewis H. Lapham, an oil pioneer who was part of the Texas Company. The steamship line was profitable from the start and greatly boosted by World War I. Harold was surely an investor in both companies, and George Dearborn, a tough businessman, grew enormously rich. He visited the Sewalls with his wife, Bessie, and they fell in love with Small Point. Harold was delighted to sell them a beachfront parcel just south of his camp.

George Dearborn owned a 189-foot steam-powered yacht named *Colonia*, reputed to have a crew of twenty-five, so he could be expected to make a stir in quiet, low-keyed Small Point. Built in 1915, his camp was of one story, clad in slabs to look like a log cabin. It was extensive, with separate guest cottages and one for the boys, another for servants, a greenhouse, and a laundry. Rural electric service was in the distant future, so an electric generator house was included, and a massive two-level garage to house Mr. Dearborn's automobile collection. A pump house was constructed on the pond. The estate was to be known as "Camp Seguin," but the name did not stick.

The builder was William H. Gilman of Phippsburg, father of the local historian of the same name, and another example of Maine men having multiple skills, nearly always including construction. They built their own houses. Abner Lowell—retired from the sea, becoming a farmer—was hired to complete construction of Small Point's first stand-alone schoolhouse in the year 1815.

Now, the Dearborns' "Camp Seguin" was not the way things were done at Small Point, but the Dearborns were welcomed by the community, in part because they became immediate supporters of the Small Point Club, of which George became president following the death of Joseph Fox Bodwell. He was succeeded in this office by his wife, Bessie, following his death in 1920.

Bessie Dearborn was a powerful woman. She had a taste for automobiles, like her late husband, and is said to have rented the Arthur Sewall carriage house to store vehicles that exceeded the room in her own ten-car facility. She always provided a car for the club. Legend has it that whenever a grandchild was born, Bessie would add another bedroom, so as to ensure her peace and quiet.

The Dearborns had two sons, George and Douglas. George died in 1925 without issue. Douglas married three times, having two sons by his first marriage in 1926, to Margaret Stuyvesant Wainwright, which ended in divorce in 1932. His second marriage was to Susan Breck of Small Point, the daughter of Sydney Manley and Duer DuPont Breck. They had a daughter who was named Susan Cony Dearborn and was known as Cony, there being already a number of Susans in the family.

Douglas and Susan were married in New York, at her mother's apartment at 321 East 72nd Street, Harrison Wright being one of the officiants. Mrs. Dearborn lived at 280 Park Avenue. She arranged for the newlyweds to have the apartment on the floor below hers, where she could keep an eye on them—and she did.

Mrs. Dearborn told Susan that she was not to leave the apartment alone; if she wanted to shop, she must be accompanied by Mrs. Dearborn's chauffeur. Susan was a bright, attractive, and outspoken woman, not one to be controlled by her mother-in-law. She promptly arranged with the chauffeur to be let out of the car a block or two from the building and proceeded to shop on her own. When the marriage ended, and she walked away from the wealth and social standing of Manhattan, she explained to a startled friend, "I didn't divorce Douglas, I divorced his mother."

Bessie Dearborn evidently ran through the family fortune; according to her grandson David, "There was nothing left" for his generation. The massive camp was eventually sold to John Chandler, Jr., who promptly removed the ant-infested slab siding and replaced it with cedar shingles. The Chandlers also added a saltwater swimming pool. The basic camp remains intact.

SUSAN McDOWELL

Susan Breck Dearborn subsequently married Alan McDowell, a chemical engineer, and had another daughter, Sydney, who has kindly provided me with the information about her mother's marriage to Douglas Dearborn. Susan worked for a time as a salesclerk at Bonwit Teller, a highly fashionable women's store that occupied a former mansion in Back Bay, Boston. Her infallible taste and imagination made her much sought-after in the well-known store. She was able to acquire her own house at Small Point, as utterly unlike the Dearborn Estate as one could imagine; this was the Reuben Fletcher House, located on the main road opposite what once was Sylvester's store and post office and just down from the schoolhouse. This was once the village center of Small Point, with the town landing and the Aliquippa Hotel just to the west on the harbor.

12

The Fletcher House

The Fletcher House looks like a small cape, but having only two rooms in the main block, it is correctly known as a "hall and parlor" house. A kitchen ell is somewhat later; the main block dates from 1790. The house was originally located just off the Morse Mountain Road and was part of a small farming community. In about 1820, it and the Webber House (a Federal cape) were moved to what is now Small Point Road, the Fletcher placed on the bank of an ice pond, the cape just up the road to the north. Was the move in order to take advantage of the ice trade?

Ice was a major industry in Phippsburg by the 1880s and beyond, with thousands of tons produced at sites in Sebasco and Parker's Head, and at the Center, where acres of pasture to the north of the village were made into a pond by construction of a dam. Yet Small Point ice was produced in smaller quantities and was mostly for local use, whereas the large companies shipped ice to the South and beyond. When Susan bought the Fletcher House, it had a small barn which may well have been an icehouse. That building did not survive; indeed, there are very few if any ice houses left in Maine—talk about minimal construction.

The ice pond was created by Tallman Lowell, who had a dam made near the Sylvester Store, now the route of the highway. Ice was sent to the wharf by the Aliquippa Hotel via an elaborate system of conveyor ramps manned by men with poles. The ice pond is now a marsh with salt- and freshwater mixed; a culvert runs beneath the highway. The Wyman farm also had an ice pond and icehouse, part of their facilities for support of the local community, and later the summer community.

Another essential Small Point industry was the making or "trying" of salt. Large kettles of seawater were boiled down until salt was left to be dried and used to preserve fish. This was the sole method for preparing fish for shipment. According to the Gilmans, the "Lower Saltworks" was located "near Fish House Cove." This is an early name, which was later changed to "Lobster Cove." Remains of the works are found just north of the Gun Club, near the end of the point. There must have also been a brickyard reasonably nearby.

Susan McDowell purchased the Fletcher House in October 1953 from Bertie Foard Penton, identified in the deed as "widow Penton." Born in North Carolina in 1885, she was married to George R. Penton of New York City. The Phippsburg Directory of 1936–37 shows that Small Point was their "sr" (summer residence). She died in North

The Fletcher House. (*TH*)

Carolina in 1966. The Pentons must have liked the primitive nature of the place, which lacked running water. There is no evidence of the house ever having its own well.

Transfers of property were frequent in Phippsburg, so it is not surprising that this property was at one time owned by a Lowell and by a Sylvester—two prominent local families. The Pentons had acquired the property in 1923 from Almira M. Sylvester; it was, after all, a Sylvester neighborhood. The photograph in Elin Dozois's book identifies the place as the "Dearborn-Sylvester House," though the image is older than Susan's ownership by perhaps fifty years. Almira Sylvester, no doubt, carried water from the Sylvester well across the road, as Susan did initially.

Susan loved the house, despite its limitations: it had no plumbing save a kitchen sink. Water was drawn from the dug well across the road until the founding of the Development Company in 1958, which provided a line for seasonal use. Then there was only cold running water in the kitchen and for an outdoor shower at the back. A privy in the barn was replaced by a composting toilet. Fortunately for Susan and her two daughters, the Joseph Manley Cottage, home to her brother Manley and sister Sydney, was about 1 mile away, well-equipped with indoor plumbing.

Now, another crossing of paths: Sydney McDowell had a successful career in advertising in New York and was able to keep her ties to Small Point. My aunt, Polly, had died in 1977, and in 1980, Sydney purchased the Arthur Sewall Carriage House for her use in summers. Neither she nor Cony had any use for the "Little House" as they called it, and it sat vacant for some thirty years, having only basic maintenance. A spacious covered deck that Susan added in 1970 after her brother Manley's death was near collapse, but the basic old house endured. I had always wanted to own and restore it. In 2009, Sydney's daughter, Nicole, sold it to me.

Photograph of the Fletcher House interior, the old kitchen or "hall." (*TH*)

A number of mysteries cling to the house. When it was moved, the large central chimney serving a wide kitchen fireplace and oven and a fireplace in the parlor was evidently moved intact, a new chimney foundation or "table" being constructed on the new site. Moving a massive central chimney with the house would have greatly increased the weight of the structure. Was the chimney in fact dismantled and rebuilt? The foundation table, made of two parallel stone walls topped with heavy wooden beams, was still in place when I set out to rebuild the stone foundation of the house; sadly, it was not sound enough to be re-used.

The actual central chimney and fireplaces were long gone, replaced by a small stove chimney. Removal of the chimney allowed for a small chamber to be created at the rear of the first floor. The window that was added was in the nine-over-six pattern that originally graced the five windows of the first floor, so those sashes must have been in place when the chimney was taken out, around 1840. Perhaps at this same time, the parlor was re-plastered over sawn lath, and casing with Greek Revival fluting added to windows and doors. This remodeling was highly popular in the mid-nineteenth century among owners of early houses, and we have here a modest example. Wallpaper might have seen its first use in the "new" parlor; my friend, Candice Thornton Lee, a retired interior decorator and former member of Greater Portland Landmarks Advisory Service, assured me that wallpaper would have been introduced at the time of this remodeling. Also known as the "best room," the parlor also served as the master bedroom. Children slept in the attic.

Also, how would a house have been moved in the early nineteenth century? The heavy equipment of the day was a team of oxen. For the big jobs, local farmers combined teams. The building would have been drawn over log rollers or, in winter, placed on a log sledge. In those days, it was always easier to move a building than to construct a whole new one. Maine has many examples of houses that were moved, often joined to other structures, sometimes raised a story. Nowadays, rapid demolition by machine is the rule as it is cost-effective. Salvage has become junk.

Some of the "modernizations" were unfortunate. Here the chimney removal permitted a conventional straight-run front stair, but the house did not have the depth to accommodate it. As a result, you hit your head on the sloping ceiling at the top of the stair. Lacking any evidence of the original stair, we placed a simple ladder-type at the rear, behind the reconstructed chimney. The narrow, turning stair at the front entry opposite the door is less common in Sagadahoc County, more often found in York County. People built what they were used to.

13

Summer People

The sociology of the Small Point summer community (some referred to it as a "summer colony" with all that the term implies) is complex and highly relevant to our historical journey. Whereas many such communities were started by people "from away," as in the case of Sebasco Estates, "Cliffstone" was the creation of two fellows from Maine—one a successful stone quarry operator, the other a retired seaman. They took over a small farming community and transformed the way it operated.

First, there were immediate jobs in construction, which local carpenters like Charles McIntyre were happy to take on, and there was a similarly immediate need for provisions for the new residents. In 1889, a store was opened, and its goods came from local farmers like Martin Wyman and the Spragues.

Also, the newcomers, many having large households, needed "help." This meant job opportunities for locals, mainly for women, though "caretakers" were also in demand. A class system emerged. Local people called their employers "Mr. Manley" or "Mrs. Sewall," and their employers called them (and all local residents) "Wilbur" or "Theresa." This practice was in use when I was a child at Small Point, but my generation was never called Mr. or Mrs. From that time on everyone was on a first-name basis. Yet the class system prevailed; the older generations were very much in control.

A somewhat awkward compromise that was widely adopted among the summer people was for youngsters to call their parents' friends "Uncle Manley" (we did), instead of "Mr. Breck" (too formal) or plain "Manley" (much too informal). You will still hear this use of unrelated "aunts" and "uncles." Yet for the local people, there were few exceptions to the rules.

The summer community had certain rituals, overseen by the ruling dowagers—Mrs. Percy, Mrs. Mellen, Mrs. Breck, and slightly younger but equally regal, Mrs. Trott, Mrs. Curtis, Mrs. Sewall, Mrs. Edge, and Mrs. Chandler. On a fair summer's day, the morning ritual was a visit to the beach below the club, known as "Little Beach." If the tide was low, everyone could have a swim in the river and cross to "The Big Beach" to walk or swim in the surf. It was an opportunity for the dowagers to observe and review the younger citizens, dressed as they were only in bathing suits (the older ladies wore suitably outdated black swimwear). The children generally behaved; the dogs, loose of course, often did not. Some brought picnics to the beach. It was understood that only children and servants frequented the beach in the afternoon.

If this all sounds somewhat regulated, let me tell you about parties. Gatherings on the beach at night were a favorite pastime, with beer flowing. The biggest of these happened on the Saturday night of Labor Day Weekend, hosted by the Chandler boys—Nat, Charlie, and John. A huge bonfire was the focus. The brothers led the crowd in singing, "Tis beer, tis beer that makes the world go round!"

There were in fact three parties in observance of the season's end, the most important being the fancy dress ball, held for decades at the club until the crowd became too large. Everyone attended in costume. The senior ladies were the judges, awarding prizes for the funniest, cleverest, most beautiful, etc. costumes. Family groups lined up and paraded across the living room, as Cliff Leeman and his orchestra played an appropriate tune. I remember Walter Edge (the governor of New Jersey) dressed as a bishop, with Camilla, his wife, an acolyte (I do not recall the theme). Then it was time for dancing and drinking—lots of both.

On Sunday at noon came the final volley, the whiskey sour party on the beach. Huge carboys were filled with a mix of lemon juice, sugar, cheap whiskey, and beer, easy to drink and, in the hot sun, rapidly intoxicating.

The community did not immediately shut down after all this; in those days, schools resumed in mid-September, and the club remained open. All of that changed with schools and colleges beginning in late August. The old query, "Are you here for the season?" has lost its meaning as no one is any more.

THE OTHER SIDE

"Small wonder" is a Maine expression, synonymous with "surprisingly," for example: "Uncle Henry took drunk and fell offn the dock. Small wondah he want drowned."

My Cambridge School classmate Ross Hall became a professor of linguistics at Northeastern University. I asked him if he thought the Maine dialects would disappear as people mixed more and more with outsiders, and he said "no." The dialect with which I am familiar (there are subtle variations in different areas of the state) harks back centuries. It is spoken by relatively young people as well as by old-timers. It can be more or less obvious; when I was in the hospital recently, my roommate was a fisherman from Rockland, who spoke to his mother in strong dialect, less so to the medical staff. Eugene O'Neil wrote his play *Desire Under the Elms* entirely in dialect; it is hard to read. John Cariani's *Almost, Maine* contains no dialect.

My friend, John McMann, never lost it, though he worked as an engineer in Massachusetts. He grew up in Small Point in a small house that his father (a Canadian by birth) had built on the hillside between the schoolhouse and the Fletcher House. John's father did some work for my aunt, and John tagged along which is how we became friends. Throughout the teenage years, we worked and played and drank together, Bunny Terry and I from the summer people and John and Gerald Wyman from the local community. John was hired as stage manager when the Small Point Summer School opened, and I was hired as director of the theatre program. Though he spoke in the dialect, John was able to blur the line between summer and local residents.

John's mother, Doris, worked as a cook for Dolly Jayne, and Peggy Wyman, Gerald's mother, had a catering service whereby she would come and cook dinner at your house, and she worked during the winter as a cook for the senior John Chandlers. Some local women continue to clean cottages as they have done for decades and as their mothers did.

THE DIALECT

The Maine dialect has in recent times provided the stuff of comedy, recordings entitled "Bert and I" and more recently performances by Bob Marley of "Upta Camp" fame. The dialect tends to be slow and somewhat nasal. Double negatives are common: "I ain't got no teeth," the Rockland fisherman said to a nurse. "He was up to Bath" is no doubt an old construction, as is "he took sick (or drunk)." "They used us pretty good" for "they treated us well." Also, there is "ayuh" for yes. All of these were perceived by the well-schooled summer folk as evidence of lack of education or of plain stupidity. In fact, the dialect was brought by settlers from southwestern England in the eighteenth century and survives to this day. What follows is a further, admittedly brief, sample of the dialect.

> "Never come accrost anythin like it."
> "rather or not" (whether)
> "I liketa died," or "I liketa shit" (I could have)
> "He took sick." "He took fits."
> "He was a coupla brick shorta hod."
> "He was over to the post office."
> Or exchanges: "I'm sorry that you lost your husband." "I didn't lose him, I know exactly where he is!"
> "You fillda tank?" "Yep, fillder rideupda top."
> "Where's Mabel?" "She's upta the cemetery." " Oh, planting out pansies?" "Nope, pushin up daisies."
> "How you doin?" "Oh, I'm stayin on the green sida the turf."
> As opposed to "Deadern hell."

Aunt Polly took the dialect in stride. Through her work as manager of the Small Point Club, she came to know the local families whose daughters worked there—notably the Wymans and the Bowkers, two of Phippsburg's most prominent original families. She knew that they were descendants of English settlers, her being a descendant of Loyalists who fled Boston at the time of the Revolutionary War. She knew that the Small Point people were intelligent and were not afraid of hard work.

Howard Bowker was the road commissioner and an excavation contractor—as kind and helpful a man as I have known. His wife, Helene (my aunt always called her "Mrs. Bowker"), worked for Polly as a housekeeper (my mother was annoyed to see her out helping Polly in the garden instead of cleaning the house). Come to find, Helene was also an artist who did historic views of the Center in an impressionist style, as well as any other subjects that caught her fancy. Polly and Sarah Mellen persuaded her to have an exhibit in the first floor of Polly's carriage house residence, "The Barn," and it was most successful.

My aunt was "Polly" to Raymond and Theresa Wyman, who ran the local general store and post office in the original Bodwell-era building, and to Irving and Julia Wallace, who lived in the Dearborn caretaker's cottage. Polly and Julia shared a love of horticulture, and Julia knew of old cellar holes where old roses still bloomed and a piece could be dug and transplanted.

The Wallaces' son, Don, lost his job at Bath Iron Works and was at a loss to support his family. Convinced that "he could fix anything," Polly promoted him to her friends in the summer community, and for a time, he was caretaker of our camp.

The first caretaker (in 1937) was Swanton Wyman, Raymond's older brother. Their father, Martin Wyman, told his four sons that if they chose not to remain on the family farm, he would give each one $500 to make a home somewhere else. Swanton took him up on the offer and purchased a fine old cape. Asa, Wilbur, and Raymond operated the family farm and the store. Asa and Wilbur and their only sister, Emma, occupied the Isaiah Wyman House; and Raymond and Theresa built a house next door for their large family.

Swanton and Mary Donohue Wyman (known as "Peggy") lived in the cape near the Bodwell Grange, which was originally the home of Daniel Blaisdell. They raised four boys—Swanton, Jr., George F., Martin J., and Gerald E.—and two daughters—Kathleen and Barbara. The cape must have been a lively place. They operated a farm, raising turkeys and two pigs every year. An orchard supplied apples and pears, and a huge planting of rhubarb once yielded a crop of 600 lb, according to Gerald.

In 2013, we sold the Charles Hinkle Camp. By a remarkable coincidence, the Blaisdell Farm came on the market, and we bought it. We immediately started to prune the apples and to rescue the rhubarb from weeds and underbrush. To be living where the Wymans once lived is a deeply moving experience for me. Both George and Gerald have visited and reminisced. George spotted a horizontal timber in the barn, which he said Swanton had cut and trimmed, and from which he hung the carcasses of freshly slaughtered hogs.

We believe that the Blaisdell House was built about 1810. Deeds show that it was owned by Thomas Alonso Pye. The Pye family came to Small Point in the 1850s and became a prominent local family. Ralph Pye, a fisherman, owned the Webber House, which was moved at the same time as the Fletcher House. He was one of the last owners of the Aliquippa, his tenure being enhanced by his wife's excellent cooking. Charles and Dorothy Pye lived on the shore of Back Bay next to the Thompson House and built the Lobster House Restaurant next door. Dot Pye was another well-known Small Point cook.

Jerusha Pye, the widow of Thomas Alphonso Pye, sold the property in 1911 to Thomas Spence, who sold it in 1927 to John and Emma Howarth. In 1930, it was acquired by Swanton Wyman. The house is not mentioned in the Gilmans' history, nor in any other published source that I know of.

The Blaisdell House has been extensively altered, with the central chimney removed, though fireplace surrounds remain in the old kitchen and the parlor. The extreme width of the surround in the old kitchen indicates that the house had a traditional kitchen fireplace with bake oven—a feature that went out of fashion in the early nineteenth century when iron stoves became available. This important clue as to the age of the house is not borne out by other evidence. Window openings are clearly for six-over-six sash, suggesting a date of 1820 or later.

Original plaster, over sawn lath, is largely intact. Rather than strip wallpaper, previous owners chose to add a layer of fiberboard, on which more paper was hung. At that time, the curiously narrow door casings were replaced by 4-inch pine boards. Then came another layer, this time drywall, and more paper. Recently, yet another layer of drywall, this time fastened with 2.5-inch screws. We have stripped the fireplace wall of the old kitchen down to the plaster, and I am painting a Rufus Porter-style mural on it.

Interior doors have four panels but only two doors match; the hallway to parlor door and the parlor to study door have raised panels both sides and plain styles and rails. The hallway to living room (old kitchen) door has raised panels with molded styles and rails, and flat panels on the other side. The doors have clearly been cut down to fit the openings. These inconsistencies strongly suggest that the house was built using salvage from an earlier house.

To the north of our property is a cellar hole. Could a house on that site have been demolished, and the parts used in the Blaisdell cape? So far, I have found no clues. Maybe this book will shake some loose. Some 200 years ago, no old materials went to waste.

Two somewhat oversized gabled dormers were added to the front. The white picket fence is gone, but many shrubs and perennials—some no doubt planted by Peggy—survive and flourish. I am struck by the fact that we had at camp a mock orange shrub and white *iris siberica*, both of which are growing at the Blaisdell Farm. Did Swanton and Peggy offer transplants?

History is marked by paths that cross.

The Daniel Blaisdell Farm in 2020. (*TH*)

Daniel Blaisdell Farm, *c.* 1940. (*Courtesy of Gloria Gray*)

TEMPERANCE AND INTEMPERANCE

In 1851, the Maine legislature passed a law forbidding the sale of alcoholic beverages of any kind. Governor Neil Dow of Portland, who became a general in the Union Army, was a fanatical and ceaseless advocate of temperance. The law was rescinded shortly after, then reinstated, remaining on the books until 1933.

Now, before we condemn the temperance movement altogether, as hysterical and senseless (Prohibition did not work), we should consider the use of alcohol, particularly rum, in the years before Maine, followed by a number of states, took seemingly drastic action. The following is from Luann Yetter's *Portland's Past*, published by the History Press:

> In the early part of the 1800s, rum was pervasive in the city's social life. Every grocery store provided a cask from which customers could serve themselves. During gatherings such as military musters, vendors would sell gingerbread, molasses candy and rum punch, not just to the men but to the women and children in the crowd as well. Rum was served at agricultural fairs, firemen's parades, cattle shows, and even town meetings. Rum was even sold inside the courthouse. At eleven o'clock in the morning, a bell would ring in Portland, and laborers would take a break with salt fish, crackers and rum.... At sea, navy and merchant sailors counted on their daily rum ration.[1]

When the Small Point Club opened in 1897, it was hardly totally "dry." Members gathered in the evening for conversation and drinks. Where exactly the liquor came from, I cannot say. Massachusetts was never bound by such a state statute. The club provided a cabinet with individual lockers in which the men could store their supplies. Some of the doors were marked with initials: O. E. B. for Orville Baker, J. F. B. for Joseph Fox Bodwell, and S. C. M. for Samuel Cony Manley. The cabinet remains in use today, for liquor storage, by the club.

After the repeal of national Prohibition, the laws in Maine were decided by each city and town. Until 1970, Phippsburg sold no liquor, only beer in stores. I was shocked to be shown a wine list at the club, and to attend a fully catered wedding rehearsal dinner at the Lobster House. Local theory has it that the elderly ladies in town, who controlled the vote, gradually died off.

The laws regarding alcoholic beverages had a long evolution in Maine. Following Prohibition, the sale of spirits and wines has exclusively handled by the state, through a network of state liquor stores. These stores had all the charm of a public lavatory. There was no decoration, no advertising, and no displays. On the wall above a counter was a printed list of items available. The customer filled out the item number on a separate slip for each item and handed the slips to a uniformed clerk behind the sales counter. The clerk then gathered your order, wrapping each bottle in plain paper with a piece of tape to seal it, putting the bottles into a bag or box, and collecting your payment in cash. State stores continue in New Hampshire, generating a good portion of the state's revenue from huge discount stores; they are full of advertising and displays. Maine continued operating state stores until around 2000, but grocery stores and supermarkets, known as "Agency Stores," had become the convenient sources; now, we also have stores selling only wines and spirits and are actively competing in the trade.

Cocktails were always a fixture of Small Point social life. That is not to say that people were particular about what they drank. Nowadays, there is considerable interest in fancy (expensive) drinks—not so years ago. Bellows Partners' Choice was a favorite—a dreadful, cheap blended whiskey guaranteed to give one a headache next morning. For gin, there was locally produced Poland Spring Gin, sold in a green figural bottle of an old man with a staff, probably worth more than its contents, and found today in antiques shops. My parents liked "Old Fashioneds," made with Old Thompson blend, a maraschino cherry, and maybe a slice of lemon. Only a few families served wine with dinner.

At the club, guests continued to furnish their own spirits (and to use the cabinet) until around 2005, when the state liquor commission told management that the practice was illegal. Since then, we have had a bartender, which is in fact convenient, and the drinks are reasonably priced. A few members squawked at first, but they soon decided not to spend cocktail hour upstairs in their rooms.

Cocktail hour at the club is a time to renew old friendships and make new ones. Members come from all over the country to stay, making up a community strangely separate from the resident summer folk, some of whom seem unaware that "people stay at the Club."

14

Military History

No battles have been fought on Small Point soil—none of a military nature, that is. Small Point men actively participated in every war involving the United States and leading to its creation. Daniel Blaisdell's name appears on the record of veterans of the Revolutionary War as one entitled to certain benefits. The War of 1812 drew soldiers from Small Point and saw the first use of Morse's Mountain as a lookout.

Samuel Cony, Joseph Manley's father-in-law, served as governor during the Civil War, and he was responsible for more than 70,000 men joining the Union forces. Records are inconsistent, but it is clear that more than 9,000 of these soldiers perished, more from disease than in combat. The war was hideous beyond belief. There are hundreds of books about the Civil War. This is not one of them.

Two members of the Fletcher family served in the Union Army, and at least two top officers had Small Point connections, most notably General Thomas W. Hyde. Born in 1841, Hyde had a lively career in the army, starting as a member of the Seventh Maine Volunteer Infantry Regiment, receiving a number of promotions. He took part in the Second Battle of Bull Run, the Battle of Antietam (for which he was awarded the Medal of Honor), and the Battle of Gettysburg. He was present at Lee's surrender in 1865.

General Hyde was due to be promoted to Brigadier General, but he declined and returned to Bath after the war and served three terms in the Maine Senate beginning in 1873. In 1878, he was elected mayor of Bath. He was to prove at least as able in business as he had been in the military.

He started the Hyde Windlass Company, a foundry making metal parts for wooden ships, and soon decided to get into ship-building. In 1884, he founded Bath Iron Works and built a pair of Navy gunboats out of steel.

Thomas Hyde's son, John, commissioned Portland's premier architect John Calvin Stevens to design his splendid estate on southern High Street. He called it "Elmhurst." Now, it functions as the Hyde School. The main building appears largely intact with its sweeping drive and *porte-cochère*, but the tall iron fence is in shameful disrepair, no doubt reflecting the school administration's philosophical disdain for fences, and the tendency for educational institutions to pay little heed to historic preservation. The fence has been removed, except for the main gateway.

The general was, of course, a friend of the Manleys and the Small Point political and social crowd. He often visited Small Point, where his daughter, Eleanor Hyde Phillips, later purchased the Harding Cottage, renaming it "Hesperus" because "it was a wreck when I bought it." Period photographs show the general at the beach, wearing his high silk hat.

ELEANOR PHILLIPS

Mrs. Phillips as she was always known was truly a *grande dame* of Small Point. She dressed elegantly, always wearing a hat when outdoors, accompanied always by her brown poodle named Echo. In the tradition of young ladies born to wealth, she had traveled in Europe. She studied music with the renowned Nadia Boulanger, becoming an accomplished soprano. She performed in recitals in Boston—of course, she never performed with an opera company; that would have been considered vulgar. Her Bath neighbor Emma Eames did so and became famous. Eleanor played the piano at the club for Sunday services, singing robustly in her aging, quavering voice.

The hymns were generally robust. "Onward, Christian Soldiers" was a favorite, as was "Goldern Harps Are Sounding" with its polka-like rhythm:

All his work is ended;
Joyfully we sing,
Jesus is ascended!
Glory to the king!

The Navy hymn "Eternal Father, Strong to Save" might be called the Small Point Anthem. There were Navy veterans present, the community subscribing to the belief that the Navy was the elite branch of the service. The hymn reflects the anxiety of an earlier time when those who traveled by ship were indeed subject to "peril on the sea." They were jolly good hymns in the British tradition. Quieter ones like "Abide with Me" might have been included in occasional Sunday evening "Hymn-sings." When Mrs. Phillips became too old to drive safely, as several minor accidents attested, John McMann and George Wyman became her chauffeurs.

Mrs. Phillips's house, the Harding Cottage, was built in 1898 for Henry McLennan Harding of Bath. Following the construction of the club by a year, it was the first cottage built on Club Road, south of the club. Harding's brother, Edward, an architect in New York City, helped to design the cottage with its unusual octagonal main block and the kitchen on a lower level. Edward Harding also designed the Patten Free Library in Bath. Clearly, the Maine connection was maintained.

Henry Harding had first visited the site with his father, on occasion camping there. The family stayed at the Rutledge Hotel in Popham and would hire a carriage to take them to Small Point via Seawall Beach, crossing Morse's and Sprague's Rivers. Careful knowledge of the tide was required. Prior to the cottage, they had a bath house constructed near the beach by Charles McIntyre, Small Point's leading contractor. It was evidently lost in a storm but is shown in old photographs.

There are no known photographs of the footbridge that Henry Harding designed and built to cross the Sprague River. A pair of bolts set into the ledge below the site of the Anderson Cottage mark the west end of the bridge; the absence of ledge on the other shore no doubt contributed to the demise of the bridge, perhaps during the winter following its construction. Joseph Bodwell indicated in publicity for "Cliffstone" that bridges would be built across both rivers. It did not happen.

In 1948, the cottage was sold to Norman von Post Schwab, who was apparently responsible for the "wreck" that greeted Eleanor Phillips. After her death, the property was acquired by Harrison Hoffman, grandson of Harrison Wright—another crossing of paths.

The other Civil War officer with important Small Point ties was Colonel Benjamin Franklin Watson. Originally from Lawrence, Massachusetts, he was active in government, editor and owner of the *Lawrence Sentinel*, and postmaster. Trained in the law, he practiced in Massachusetts courts until the outbreak of the war.

The "Massachusetts Sixth," of which he was major, was the first unit summoned by President Lincoln to defend the city of Washington. When the regiment reached Baltimore, it did not march through the streets but boarded trolleys of the day, known as horsecars, hoping to avoid "inciting the angry Southern elements of the population." This did not exactly work out, and the carriages were attacked by a "dense and abusive crowd." A shot was fired at the soldiers whereupon the colonel gave the order to return fire and "this detachment unquestionably shed, and drew from their opponents, the first blood of the war. The regiment reached the railway station and were transported to the Capital to report to General Scott and the President."

The quotations above are from a letter to the editor of *The Evening Post* (of New York) by William Hays Ward, dated 1905, the year of Watson's death. Watson had moved to New York after the war. How did he come to know Small Point? A possible clue is his origin in Lawrence; Joseph Bodwell had his first career there working with granite on the immense factory buildings. I find no other connections to Maine. Col. Watson retired from the practice of law in 1892.

15

Sources

The Bodwell Cottage was inherited by Bodwell's wife, Hannah, and their son, Joseph Fox Bodwell. There was apparently some difficulty in settling the estate of Gov. Bodwell; in 1897, a committee of partition appointed by the Supreme Judicial Court of Maine drew a line north to south from opposite Spinney's Inn, with the Bodwell heirs getting the eastern portion and Spinney the less valuable western strip. In 1892, Hannah and Joseph sold the cottage and an adjacent lot to Col. Watson. An additional lot, on the harbor side of the town road, was conveyed to Watson in 1900.

The pursuit of history leads one into surprises. Paths cross unexpectedly. Elisabeth Trott was, I thought, an unpleasant and controlling woman, quite tall and intimidating to a child like me. Her husband, Ray, was shorter and much more genial. Their daughter, Libby, was guilty of building a camp on the rocks below the cliff at the end of Club Road, in an area shown as common land for "Cliffstone" residents. After Bodwell's death, those common areas went into private ownership, which complicated the matter considerably.

Elisabeth was a force to be reckoned with. She was also an historian. Eventually, Libby and I became friends and she passed along to me an amazing collection of her mother's photographs, notes, and newspaper clippings; Elisabeth subscribed to the Bath paper and the *New York Times*, so we poor folk from Boston were omitted. Here is a fascinating, puzzling, typical line from her notes on Small Point houses: "Sumner & Elena Sewall—old Manson cottage—"Blue Cottage" Was built 18—by Geo Manson a lawyer from Boston—Was a tavern? Serves liquor [illeg.] Hunt, Lowell?"

The house likely predates Manson; its use as a tavern would have been much earlier, when, as she observes, there were "three old houses at bend of road—lilac bushes," in short, a little village with the Sprague and Sylvester houses nearby—how I wish she had written a finished history. Elisabeth was a Houghton from Bath; her grandfather, Levi Houghton, was a noted shipbuilder. The Trott Cottage, built in 1929, contains paneling of wide boards from the Levi Houghton House in Bath, which was demolished to provide parking space for Bath Iron Works. Raymond Trott was also descended from a Bath ship-builder. He became a bank president in Providence. The Trotts had previously rented the Foltz Cottage for five summers.

Elisabeth understood the value of newspaper clippings. Weddings and obituaries are full of genealogical information, as are her sometimes illegible notes. Also, historic documents can be inconsistent or contradictory—see the reference to Sumner Sewall as a member of the "Lafayette Quadrille." Ancestry.com often gives different birth or death dates for a person. So, we must be willing to compare sources and frankly reveal contradictions, including our own blunders. I am guilty of identifying the Bodwell Cottage as having been built by Col. Watson, its second owner, in the *Centennial History of the Small Point Club*. A Maine trade publication of the late nineteenth century, *The Industrial Journal*, printed news about buildings like the club that appears to be essentially unchecked material furnished by the builders.

Even architects' drawings seldom correspond to exactly what was built. The club has a simpler exterior treatment (and fewer rooms than reported in the *Industrial Journal*). Still, the set of plans and elevations, discovered in the attic and promptly framed, are a valuable resource.

Plans for the Foltz Cottage at the end of Club Road are likewise preserved at the cottage. They show a covered veranda extending around the east and south sides, overlooking the view of the beach and the ocean, perhaps the best views in the community. The south veranda was not covered but left an open deck, and a three-sided bay at the corner was omitted. On the first floor, the cottage was finished like a camp. Framing was left exposed, stained a dark color, with the walls not finished in plaster. A deep inglenook of high-backed benches flanked the fireplace in the parlor. Bedrooms on the second floor were plastered, much like those of the nearby club. In the plan, the house was a simple rectangle, with a height of two and a half stories and a gambrel roof.

Dr. J. Clinton Foltz was an army surgeon in World War I. The house was designed by George T. Pearson, an architect from Schenectady, New York, where the Foltz resided. After his death in 1943, the cottage passed to his daughter, Polly Foltz Bentley. She was not financially able to afford it, so she rented it to the Trott family and others, taking in boarders when she was there, but finally sold the place.

The new owners were Robert Charles and his wife, Olive Evans, the daughter of Ellena Sewall by her first husband. The Charleses—a charming, gracious couple whose children were my friends—found the dark Victorian interior not to their liking. This was the late 1960s, when Victorian was not cool at all. At the club, for example, Janey Sewall, the New York decorator, had the varnished woodwork painted light gray and the floral wallpaper replaced with white paint.

The Foltz Cottage suffered a more drastic remodeling; the veranda to the east of the parlor was entirely combined with the parlor, a somewhat alarming structural feat that left the second-floor exterior wall suspended without a single post. The spaces between the veranda posts were filled with plate glass, giving an unbroken expanse of the spectacular view, and creating a space without ventilation that was so hot in the morning sun as to be avoided altogether. The inglenook was taken out, making that side of the parlor more accessible. The dining room remained dark and cool, with its screened veranda intact. That room was the scene of countless hilarious dinners, thanks to my dear friend Elena Charles Riley. The Foltz Cottage remains basically intact with new owners; that exterior wall could easily be replaced. Victorian is cool again.

Chase Mellen, Junior, known as "Junie," was injured in World War I and appeared at Small Point with a wooden leg (which he would simply remove when at the beach, a source of fascination for us kids). His wife was Sarah Brisbane, daughter of Arthur

Foltz Cottage. (*TH*)

Chase Mellen, Jr. and Sarah B. Mellen. (*Coll. TH*)

Brisbane, the newspaper publisher. The Mellens were entitled to spend a block of the summertime at the Manley Cottage, but they wanted their own place. Seeing that the club had closed because of wartime, Junie set out to acquire the building, planning to either remove the topmost story or demolish the building altogether. He began seeking out the shares of inactive members and had obtained a number of them when he was confronted by a committee that included my mother and Barbara Terry, determined to preserve the club. They met with Junie over martinis at the closed club. At first, he was furious, but he consented to sell back the shares that he had bought and to drop the matter. In 1946, the club reopened with Barbara Terry as manager (and board president).

Junie and Sarah Mellen were able to purchase the Bodwell Cottage from Frank and Rebecca McLanathan. The McLanathan family had inherited it from Colonel Watson. Having secured a Small Point venue of his own, Junie gave his interest in the Manley Cottage to his first cousin, Anne ("Nancy") Mellen Ijams, as a wedding present. The year was 1945. The war was over.

Legend has it that Junie Mellen assumed that his tax would increase if he increased the footprint of the house, so he set out to expand the house by altering the attic to make a third floor with bedrooms suitable for children and servants. The verandas at the sides were heavily altered and enclosed. An ugly concrete retainer was constructed across the front and filled to the level of the former veranda. Also, though the main block was unchanged, the cottage lost most of what was left of its period detail and character, and the long shed dormers spoiled the lines of the roof, which once had an observation deck at its center.

Newspaper photograph of Nancy Mellen. (*Trott coll. LH*)

The interior was modified to suit current tastes; the front and back parlors were combined, with the two corner fireplaces replaced by one with exposed brick surround and mantel. This did not cause structural damage despite removal of an entire interior partition. The dining room appears to be original. The enclosed verandas provide pleasant indoor spaces, except that Junie had both spaces enclosed in casement windows set about 4 feet above the floor; when you are seated, you do not see any view. Also, the Bodwell Cottage would have had a good, distant view of the beach and ocean, before the oak trees were allowed to grow. Let us just say that neither Junie nor Sarah had any visual sense, but the Bodwell Cottage was no palace to begin with.

In 1980, Peter and Elena Vandervoort purchased the Bodwell Cottage and adjoining lot from Abigail Mellen, who retained the lot across the highway. Elena was the former Elena Drake of the Bath family; her father was the insurance agent for many Small Point families. Elena has a keen visual sense.

The 1946–47 alterations to the cottage had an unexpected benefit for me. My mother's best friend from Canada, Embree Osler, was staying with us with her son, Alan. He was probably eleven or twelve in 1947; he was what the Canadians call a clever lad and a wee bit of a carpenter to boot. He noticed the pile of discarded lumber at the Mellen house and announced, "We're going to build a house." In the woods belonging to our neighbor Elizabeth Pattee, Alan spotted four spruce trees about 6 feet apart in a rough square—the posts for our house. Using a wheelbarrow, we transported salvage lumber to the site and nailed up four walls and a roof, Alan doing most of the carpentry. I was allowed to finish driving some of the nails if I could hit them squarely with the hammer. I was to drive many a nail after that. You might say that this was my first house.

A few years later, I had learned a little more about construction. With Bunny Terry and other friends, I set about building a driftwood shanty on Split Beach, within sight of Mrs. Edge's "Gun Club." Mrs. Edge gave us permission to do so but regretted it when she saw us making the hut more or less watertight by means of tar paper. "I wasn't expecting tar paper!" she exclaimed. I believe we spent a single night in our new beach house. Once summer was over, Mrs. Edge's caretaker, Walter Mosher, was instructed to burn the place to the ground. Likewise, the Alan Osler structure disappeared during the winter months.

When I was sixteen, I built a real house—a one-room camp, 10 × 12 feet, which I subsequently enlarged. It is still extant with numerous additions and now owned by the Ballard family.

Most of the Small Point cottages remained largely intact, some with additions and the expected modern kitchens and bathrooms "Merrymeeting," the Patten Cottage later owned by the Wright family, fell victim to the dilemma of a large family, no branch of which was able to assume ownership. So, like my grandmother's cottage, it was demolished. The descendants of Harrison Wright kept the guest cottage known as "the Bungalow" (site of the infamous deck), the carriage house, and the guest cottage up on the rise across the road; some were able to build nearby. The carriage house was acquired by Roger Farrington and Colleen Babson, remodeled into a comfortable, year-round dwelling.

The Aliquippa was vacant and in need of repair when Stephen Foote, an architect, purchased it in 1980. Following its demise as a resort, it had served as a summer camp for children, a tough situation for any building. With all of its various additions, it contained some 20,000 square feet. Mr. Foote set about making it a practical summer residence, or, specifically, two summer residences.

It is regrettable that this important early hotel could not have found a more appropriate and less compromising use. At the same time, it may be argued that it was in imminent danger of being demolished, as the Square House was, and "Merrymeeting."

Two more Small Point houses were deliberately destroyed by members of the summer community. Both were significant, early examples, not cottages. The "Square House" overlooking the harbor was built in the 1790s by members of the Lowell family, which was responsible for Lowell's Hotel, later renamed "The Aliquippa." The house had had numerous alterations to the interior, which were cleverly overcome by the efforts of Carolyn Mattison, a designer from Connecticut who rented the place for many summers before buying the entire Aliquippa property and moving into an unattractive camp built by the Varian family, which commanded a splendid harbor view, and which also yielded to her skilled touch.

Carolyn sold off "The Square House" and the Aliquippa. "The Square House" had two owners prior to the current one, who complained that the ceilings were too low. He refused offers of help in relocating the house, so he had it demolished. There were protests and newspaper coverage as far away as the *Boston Globe*. Yet the house is gone, and once gone, a historic property is gone forever, hence the importance of historic preservation.

Phippsburg passed a demolition ordinance requiring review by a historic preservation commission, but with no power to halt demolition, only to delay it for forty-five days. A full ordinance is in draft form, progressing slowly and uncertainly toward a vote by town meeting. There can be controversy over such a set of regulations, opponents stating categorically that "No one is going to tell me what to do with my house!" or worse still, "A bunch of goddam summer people aren't going to tell me what I can or can't do!" There is currently only one seasonal resident member of the commission, and there are in place numerous restrictions having to do with shoreland, suitability for septic systems, setbacks, and the like.

The truth is that the regulations would apply only to historic buildings and sites identified as "significant" in a town-wide survey and subsequently made part, by vote of the citizens, of an historic district or labeled as individual historic properties (local landmarks) worthy of preservation. Phippsburg residents who own designated historic buildings would not be affected at all, unless they wanted to alter or destroy them.

The second loss was the Thompson House by the Back Bay, which dated from about 1830. It was timber-framed and generally sound, with a front of pleasing Greek proportions facing the road and a kitchen ell at the left rear. The Thompsons were an early Small Point family, if not one of the first settlers. When I was a child, Albert Thompson was the road commissioner. His son, Warren, worked at Wyman's Store. Another son, John, lived alone in the house until his death in 2005. The new owners, part of an established Small Point summer family, gave the building to the fire department for a training site; it was duly burned to the ground and every trace of debris promptly removed. The owners did not replace the house with a new one. Greater Portland Landmarks sent members of its advisory service, who documented the Thompson House.

Ghost. (Painting, TH)

MORSE'S MOUNTAIN

On a quiet summer afternoon in 1927, George C. St. John, headmaster of Choate School in Connecticut, sat in a rocker on the veranda of the Small Point Club and gazed at the vast stretch of Seawall Beach and the forests rising behind it. "Who owns all that land?" he wondered.

Much of the Morse's Mountain land had reverted to the various branches of the Morse family following the demise of the Mountain and Seashore Company. A small number of lots had new owners. George St. John set his sights on the whole mountain, and he succeeded. In addition to creating and running Choate for an incredible forty years, he was a successful developer of Jupiter Island in Florida. He had the means. In 1938, he had a Prairie-style house constructed at the far end of a tortuous dirt road built by the Army. The architect was Edwin B. Goodell, Jr., of Boston, who had probably done commissions at Choate.

Goodell, a 1917 graduate of M.I.T., was a remarkably versatile architect; the buildings at Choate would have been in the traditional "colonial" style that one expects to find at a school, but he is best known for the 1934 Field House in Weston, Massachusetts—one of the earliest examples of the International style, predating the work of Gropius. The Prairie style was developed in Chicago by Frank Lloyd Wright. Wright favored flat roofs, whereas the roofs of the St. John House are low-pitched, which is better for Maine. It is otherwise a pure example.

In 1942, Mr. St. John's tenure of the mountain was interrupted by World War II. The Army cleared the summit of the mountain, and a radar station, one of the first,

The George St. John Cottage, "Nephelcocyggia" (*TH*)

was installed. Three low buildings and a radar tower were built at the summit, while the soldiers' barracks were located at a lower level, amid the forest. My father's friend, Frank Evans, was stationed there and remembered the hike in winter from barracks to duty as the coldest he ever experienced.

A wooden gate topped with barbed wire was placed at the end of the access road, a second one at the Sprague Marsh, and a railroad-style crossing barrier and guard house was located by the road to the barracks. The summit was protected by several machine gun emplacements made of sandbags with wooden tops covered in camouflage. After the war, all of this construction and fortification was simply abandoned in place.

The radar installation at Morse's Mountain was an innovation that enhanced the existing coastal defense system of so-called fire control towers. These tall, concrete structures were sited every few miles along the coast and served as observation posts for spotting submarines (which had to surface at least once a day). The towers were in communication with artillery batteries, the nearest being at Fort Baldwin in Popham. That tower is extant, as is the one at Bald Head in Small Point. There were no armaments located at the towers.

For the German military, the submarine was the sole weapon that could get close to the American shoreline without immediate detection. As such, they posed a real threat; in fact, the last U.S. warship to be sunk by a German submarine—the USS *Eagle PE- 56* was lost off the coast of Cape Elizabeth. The submarine was sunk days later off Block Island (article in Portland Press Herald by David Sharp, AP). Traces of war continue to appear. In 1970, Richard Lee and Herb McIntyre, returning from a fishing expedition, spotted a large, black mine bumping against the ledges of Bald Head. The Coast Guard responded and detonated the mine, causing a huge explosion.

The next military installation at Small Point continued the defense against enemy submarines. On June 21, 1960, Camilla Edge transferred an eighth of an acre at the south tip of the Point to the United States Government, where the navy set up a rake station, with another one underway at Popham. By triangulation, the two metal towers could set a target for aircraft carrying smoke bombs and observe the accuracy of the strike. This was during the Cold War; the imaginary submarines were Russian.

Access was provided by the newly-constructed Navy Road, which went south from the bend at the Williams Cottage driveway to the end of the Point. I remember vans passing our driveway, carrying uniformed personnel to the site.

In the 1980s, the metal tower was replaced by a concrete silo-type tower, and some non-military use continued, including the study by M.I.T. of continental drift (before GPS was common). Then the title was returned to Camilla Edge's heirs—the Lee and MacFadyen families. They placed a conservation easement on the entire Point, including Fuller Rock, protecting the land forever.

The Lees and MacFadyens had the concrete tower and all traces of the government uses removed, except the foundation piers of an earlier (possibly World War I-era) military structure. So, today, the whole area is in a more or less natural state. A case could be made that the tower had some historic importance and should be retained and allowed to decay naturally, but the two families deserve enormous credit for preserving a beautiful (and highly valuable) space.

George St. John was aware of the possibility that the Morse's Mountain land might be considered for either a state or a national park. At least, this was a fear shared by members of the summer community; I know of no actual proposal. Yet here were over 600 acres of largely undeveloped and highly dramatic coastal land. His solution was to divide the property into large parcels on which substantial summer dwellings would be constructed, thereby driving up the market value of the whole. This course of action turned out to be unnecessary as the St. John family came up with a brilliant and magnanimous alternative, the Morse Mountain Preserve, administered by Bates College.

The St. John family retains three historic houses for use by the several branches, as well as several seasonal rentals and one year-round early cape. The largest Army structure at the summit was lost to fire.

LOCAL CHARACTERS

Dr. St. John, who took over the Sunday services at the club from Mr. Wright, is remembered as a Small Point character—a person who stood out. There were several others, including Eleanor Phillips.

Jimmy Heald is shown in a *c.* 1915 school photograph taken outside the Center School. The Heald family lived on the Center Pond, between the road and the shore, at the bend (before the road was widened). He is perhaps ten years old. He subsequently suffered a bout of pneumonia with high fever that resulted in brain damage. Jimmy was a rugged fellow who worked as a laborer for local contractors. It was said that if Jimmy was digging a ditch, he would need to be watched, lest the ditch become deeper as it progressed. He worked to clear the site of our camp and was about to chop down an oak tree, which my parents wanted to keep. He was stopped, but ironically, my mother complained for years that the tree was shading the house, and over my protests, she eventually had it removed. I planted a new one, which was over 20 feet tall when last I saw it.

Jimmy Heald later lived on a bend in the Main Road, in a tiny white house, maybe 10 square feet, but of two stories. When he was not working, he would sit outside on a bench and wave to passing motorists. We children always looked for Jimmy.

Wilbur Wyman was more or less the manager of the family store, where his sister-in-law, Theresa, served for many years as postmaster. A man of infinite patience, Wilbur endured the demands of the summer people and the pranks of their offspring; Chase Mellen would grab a popsicle from the freezer and call out to Wilbur, "Charge it to Mrs. Motley!" Wilbur knew better. The store attempted to provide everything, drinking water in heavy 5-gallon carboys, and coal in canvas totes, which Wilbur carried on his back from the truck. Our water heater was coal-fired; my mother became expert at running it.

At the back of the store was a cabinet containing a whole wheel of delicious cheddar cheese. Needless to say, tobacco products of all kinds were in demand. I remember paying twenty-eight cents for a pack of Chesterfield Kings. Wilbur spoke in the dialect, with many "ayuhs."

For many years, Wilbur also provided home delivery. Every morning at around 9 a.m., my mother would telephone the store and place an order for groceries, which would arrive before noon in a large, rectangular splint basket and which Wilbur would place on the kitchen counter. Everyone had a charge account in those days before the credit card existed. Later, when Wilbur was less active, Tom Motley was hired to deliver, the

Photograph of the store from the west. (*courtesy of CD*)

first instance of one of the summer community being hired by the Wymans. Aunt Polly was delighted.

Wyman's Store also provided three grades of gasoline—regular, high-test, and super. The service was eventually discontinued, but gallons of fuel had already seeped out of the tanks. Grey Terry and I were part of a group of potential investors in the store property, and we tested the soil by having a well dilled. The result was terrible; we abandoned the project. Yet Richard Lee, ever quiet and determined, and his cousin, Lisa Edge, set out to cure the problem. Here is Richard's account:

> We removed four tanks and 700 tons of gasoline-saturated soils which all went to South Portland for treatment. The last day of excavation we were bailing raw gas out of the pockets in the bedrock with sealed excavators and dump trucks. We had a hole big enough to bury 3 school buses. We installed 5 monitoring wells and tested them and the local private wells for 5 years after the clean up. DEP signed off on the project as a success and said that we saved the Small Point aquifers.

The store building was moved back on the lot and heavily altered to make a residence. Grey and I had thought that a store could once again thrive at Small Point. Summer people are increasingly building year-round houses.

Junie Mellen was a prominent Small Point character. Born in New York, he was the son of Chase Mellen and Lucy Manley Melllen. He was a graduate of Harvard College, where he belonged to the Porcellian Club. If there is even a faint American aristocracy, one label of membership would be the Porcellian Club, or, at Yale, Skull and Bones. Being a graduate of Groton School would also help; Junie, being a New Yorker, did not attend Groton, which catered to the Boston aristocracy.

Long active in New York politics, Junie was a man of formidable energy, much of which became focused on Small Point projects. He arranged the purchase by a group of investors of the Sprague Farm, which occupied an area from the Back Bay north to the end of a rocky point, the entire length of Sprague Road. Some shorefront properties had been previously sold off, to the Chandlers and Sargents, and there was a town landing for local fishermen. Junie knew all the fishermen and saw to it that they had a new wharf. The plan to sell lots to allow expansion of the summer community was slow to be realized, and much of the land remains vacant.

Like all good developers, he wanted to grab the best site and build his own house. Yet did he not already have the Bodwell Cottage? Yes, but the Branch House would be for his children—my friends, Abigail and Chase, and their half-brother, Michael. Junie had a saltwater pool constructed right at the shore. The project kept him busy. His children had no interest in it whatsoever, but this was no matter as Junie had a bigger project in the works.

THE SMALL POINT SUMMER SCHOOL

Junie and Sarah Mellen, like my parents, the Smiths, and others, were somewhat older when their children were born, and therefore less involved than the younger parents in the daily activities of their children, some of which were constructive, others not so. Junie and Sarah, along with Sydney Smith, sought to channel the youthful energies into productive channels at Small Point, and their vehicle was the Small Point Summer School.

The very thought of "school in summer" horrified some of the young parents, who viewed summer as a time for family activities. Junie was never deterred by opposition. The large, relatively modern, cattle barn of the Sprague Farm became the new school, with a proscenium stage added at one end, and a kitchen and veranda at the other. Win and Maurice Blair were the general contractors. It was a large, workable space. An additional building housed an aquarium for study. The Sprague residence became staff housing and a library. The school opened on a foggy day in 1959.

Subjects taught combined the academic and the existing recreations: marine biology, painting and drawing, and theatre, plus the mandatory tennis and sailing. An outside teacher was hired for biology; the rest was handled by people in the community—Sydney taught art, Billy taught sailing in little wooden prams on the back bay; and while the name of the first tennis coach escapes me, a later one, Sam Ladd, was even later president of Maine Bank and Trust.

The theatre program fell to me. I had done some shows in Polly's carriage house, starting at age thirteen, and performed in plays at the Cambridge School directed by Whitney Haley. I was not highly qualified, but I was there. The expert is the guy who knows more than anybody else in the room.

The Mellens gave me a heavily pared-down version of *A Midsummer Night's Dream*, which I filled out somewhat, not all the way. It was a community effort, there being too few older kids enrolled, but we had the talent available. Sydney's husband Billy Smith, the sailing expert, spoke the opening words: "Now, fair Hippolyta." Our opening production was well received.

Junie was president of the Summer School Corporation. Though Sydney Smith was the director of the school, Junie was ever-present, checking the wastebaskets and so on. His manner was aggressive, his voice sometimes a screech, speech laden with profanities. I found that the best way to deal with his intrusive presence was to ask for things, preferably things available in Bath or even New York. He needed to keep busy.

I worked a total of four seasons at the Summer School, and produced, in addition to *A Midsummer Night's Dream*, Shakespeare's *The Tempest*, *Hamlet*, and *Romeo and Juliet*. Our Juliet, Kaiulani Lee, went on to become a successful actress, best-known for her portrayal of Rachel Carson, a play which she also wrote. Andrew St. John (Hamlet) and Warren Motley (Romeo) had brief acting careers. Alas, by 1965, my basic troupe who filled in the leads had dispersed, and I did so too, after making a film that was a total disaster—I knew nothing about cinema, and it showed. Dolly Jane commented that "the colors were lovely." Tell that to Ted Curtis, who happened to be president of Eastman Kodak.

The Small Point Summer School continues to serve the community. The theatre program has been compromised by the shortening of the season, allowing far less time for rehearsals. When I was a child, we came to Small Point in the middle of June and did not leave until the middle of September. Now, very few in the community are "here for the season."

THE MASONS

Frank and Phyllis Mason were introduced to Small Point by the Mellens and became important members of the summer community. I first knew them when they rented a house on Bald Head.

Bald Head, to the west of the Point, was the site of some early settlements by the Wallace and other families. It was acquired by Colonel Wriston, who did not welcome kids and other intruders, so we generally stayed away. He did have rentals.

Frank was a successful artist who had studied with DuMonde at the Art Students League in New York and become the head instructor there. Phyllis Harriman was his student and the granddaughter of E. A. Harriman. She too was a splendid painter of landscapes. Frank did wonderful coastal scenes, but his true forte was the portrait. Many Small Point residents were painted by Frank. He volunteered to paint sets for our productions, most notably for *Romeo and Juliet*. The Masons had a house moved to a lot in Junie's new development, known as the Small Point Development Company.

Their young son Crispin Connery, actually by Phyllis's first marriage, but sometimes called Mason, later became president of The Small Point Club. I am happy to own a large Frank Mason beach scene, signed "Frank Mason 1959—Small Pt. Me.," which is pictured here.

Small Point never became a popular artist's location like Monhegan Island, despite equally inspiring scenes to paint. Other artists of note include Joseph Ropes (mentioned above), Ben Foster, and John Marin. Also, there were many less well-known, like myself.

Small Pt. Maine, painting by Frank Mason (*Coll. TH*)

My path led away from the theatre, and in 1992, my partner Gary urged me to try painting— pictures, that is; I had continued to do set painting and design. Needless to say, I painted houses. The tenants at Camp had left a child's easel in the attic, which I set up facing the view, and I did a small landscape. I was hooked. Naturally, I have chosen some of my paintings based upon Small Point to illustrate this book.

HOW SMALL?

Small Point is at the southernmost end of the peninsula known as Cape Small. The origin of the name "Small" has been the subject of some debate. James D. Small, doubtless a descendant, has done extensive genealogical research into the early Smalls of Maine.

Edward Small was an English entrepreneur who came to New England in 1632 and was the founder of Piscataqua, later divided into the towns of Kittery, Eliot, South Berwick, and Berwick. With Edward was his son, Francis, another entrepreneur, who purchased Ossipee (Falmouth) from the Newichawannoch Tribe, at a cost of two blankets, two gallons of rum, 2 lb of powder, 4 lb of musket balls, and twenty strings of beads. For this, he received a huge tract in western Maine in the Saco River area.

It is interesting that Francis Small helped to arm the native people who shortly after turned against him. Francis escaped and fled to New Hampshire. As I have said before, the native people had no respect for English real estate law, though as time went on the chiefs learned to play the game.

James Small states that Cape Small was named for Francis, a theory which I have encountered elsewhere, yet it does not appear that he actually lived there, his holdings, to which he eventually returned, being to the west.

I have read at least one lengthy dissertation rejecting the connection to Francis Small, claiming that "small" is in fact the adjective. This is unlikely. The word "small" is never, to my knowledge, used in geographic labeling. Instead, the word used is invariably "little." Locally, we have Little Wood Island (of which there are several along the Maine Coast) and Little Morse's Mountain, and countless other littles—an interesting topic, if not terribly important.

Small Point was less populated and therefore quieter than neighboring villages like Popham and West Point, yet the people did not want for social activities. The Bodwell Grange, named for the governor, is located across from the Wildes Farm and near the Daniel Blaisdell House. The Bodwell Grange Road originally ran past the hall and north then east to Popham. The present Popham Road intersection was constructed later.

The automobile was doubtless responsible for the gradual demise of the Grange, and of the Dromore Grange well to the north. People were getting around. Some of the last members were William Gilman, Priscilla McIntire, Win Blair, Marguerite Blair, Myrtle Pye, Margaret Wyman, Mary Pratt, Clyde Pye, Leo Hamel, William Blaisdell, and Helena Oliver. The Grange was founded in 1887 and thrived into the 1960s. The building stood vacant for many years until John's son, James McMann, purchased it, planning to create two apartments.

Equally important was the Small Point Baptist Church. Now, "Baptist" is a word that needs some context, being in Maine, not Georgia. The Baptist Church has no central organization or hierarchy, and so in Maine every church is essentially independent.

The Small Point Baptist Church prior to expansion (*TH*)

The actual services are in some ways quite similar to those of the congregational denomination, which was once synonymous with the government and allowed no other religious sects, especially Catholics. Times have changed; in some smaller towns, the Baptists and Congregationalists join together in winter, the congregation being smaller and only a single church needing to be heated.

The Baptists are theoretically followers of John the Baptizer, a cousin of Jesus, and a strict advocate of the simple life who lived in the wilderness and ate no meat. He initiated his followers by immersing them totally in the Jordan River. The notes of the Phippsburg Historical Society quote a local newspaper announcement that a baptism will take place "at Small Point Harbor." Recent expansion of the church includes a tank for baptism.

The Baptists came to Small Point in 1820. In 1828, they erected a meeting house on land given by the Gilman family. In 1892, H. B. Lowell gave a small lot for a parish house, which was gradually finished and paid for. It was demolished around 2010, having had problems with mold. The church was extensively expanded in 1999 with the addition of a parish hall and meeting space on the lower level. The alterations were done with sensitivity to the original historic structure, thankfully.

16

Farewell

After we sold the Charles Hinkle Camp, we rented Sewall Janeway's camp near Ice Box Bend, built for his mother, our friend Ceci Sewall Janeway Coates; this gave us a base from which to furnish and prepare the Daniel Blaisdell Farm for our occupancy. Then the day came to move out and move on.

I drove to the end of Seal Cove Road and traversed its length, remembering the people I had known along the way who were no longer living: Camilla Edge, Marty and Candy Owen, Irving and Julia Wallace, Douglas and Marcia Dearborn, John Chandler, Loyal "Sag" and Janey Sewall, Sewall Williams, Nat Chandler, Ray and Elisabeth Trott, Carolyn King, Elizabeth Pattee, Fred and Helen Greene, Sybil and Osborne Coates, and Aunt Polly. All in some way belonged to my past, my path, and that is only on the road where we used to live. In a real sense, we left the summer community on that day.

We are part-time, year-round residents of Phippsburg, happy to have our early house, with central heat. Camp was fine, on a sunny August day. It is now the gathering place of the younger set; that big living room is great for parties. Here is another crossing of paths: the new owner is Arden Mason, son of Frank and Phyllis, now married to Terry Windhorst, daughter of Sally Terry Graves. The land to the immediate north of the Blaisdell Farm (with the cellar hole) belongs to Crispin Connery's son, Cabot, grandson of Phyllis.

Endnotes

CHAPTER 1

1 Guest Register, The Small Point Club (Patten Free Library, Bath).

CHAPTER 3

1 Sewall, E., *The Rivers and Marshes of Small Point* (Privately printed, *c.* 1906).

CHAPTER 5

1 Plan of Fort St. George (Maine Historical Society, Image 7542).

CHAPTER 6

1 Clark, C., *The Eastern Frontier* (New York, Knopf, 1970), pp 70–71.
2 Duncan, R. F., *Maine Coast* (New York Norton, 1992), p. 52.

CHAPTER 8

1 Rybczynski, W. *A Clearing in the Distance* (New York, Scribner 1999, chapter 6).

CHAPTER 10

1 Haviland, "Tragic Mistake... (article)," *The Working Waterfront*, pub. by Island Institute (June 2017).
2 Unsigned document, Col. Watson's inn (1962).
3 Coates, S., holiday message (*c.* 1987).

CHAPTER 11

1 Kelly, D., pages from an autobiography, provided for inclusion in this Book.

CHAPTER 13

1 Yetter, L., *Portland's Past* (Charleston. The History Press), pp. 72–73.

Bibliography

Clark, C. E., The Eastern Frontier, *The Settlement of Northern New Englsnd, 1610–1763* (New York: A. Knopf, 1970)

Coates, S., *Notes on Small Point in Early Days—1900* (Narrative in a holiday greeting, *c.* 1987)

Deed, Frank W. McLanathan and Rebecca w. McLanathan to Sarah Brisbane Mellen, 24 October 1945

Dozois, E., *Phippsburg* (Charleston, Arcadia Publishing, 1999)

Duncan, R. F., *Coastal Maine* (New York, W. Norton, 1992)

Gilman, S. and M., *Small Point, "The Cape of Many Islands"* (Phippsburg Historical Society, 1965)

Gray, G., *Small Point, Volume I* and *Small Point, Volume II* (published by the author, 2017, 2019)

Haviland, W. A., *The Tragic Mistake Made by Maine's First European Colony* (The Working Waterfront, Rockland, The Island Institute, June 2017)

Industrial Journal (trade newspaper), (Augusta, late nineteenth–early twentieth century) Excerpts provided by Earle Shettleworth, director, Maine Historic Preservation Commission.

Isaacson, D. et al., *Phippsburg—Fair to the Wind* (Phippsburg Historical Society, 1965)

Northend, M., *Historic Homes of New England* (New York, Little, Brown & Co., 1914)

Phippsburg Tax Rosters, 1794 and *1795* (Kept by Isaiah Wyman, Tax Collector, courtesy of Carol Wyman Doughty)

Rolde, N., *Maine, Downeast and Different, an Illustrated History* (New York, American Historical Press, 2006)

Sewall, A., *Message Through Time, The Photographs of Emma D. Sewall, 1836–1919* (The Harpswell Press, 1989)

Sewall, E., *The Rivers and Marshes of Small Point* (Privately printed, *c.* 1906)

Small, J. D., *Edward Small, Emigrant* (Posted online, 2001)

Small Point Club, *Original Guest Register* (beginning 1897. Patten Free Library, Bath)

Vandervoort, E., Hinkle, T. et al., *The Centennial History of the Small Point Club* (Phippsburg, The Small Point Club, Inc., 1997)

Wright, M., *Aliquippa, a History* (Phippsburg, self-published, 1989)

Yetter, L., *Portland's Past, Stories from the City by the Sea* (Charleston, The History Press, 2011)